TEEN Triple P

self-he
ook

utions

Alan
Ma

Triple P ®
Positive Parenting Program
for every parent

Published by
Triple P International Pty Ltd ABN 17 079 825 817
PO Box 1300
Milton QLD 4064
Website: www.triplep.net

Teen Triple P Self-Help Workbook
© Copyright 2009   The University of Queensland
Written by Alan Ralph & Matthew R. Sanders
ISBN 978-1-921234-86-6

Design and layout by JamToast, Brisbane.
Cover and text design by Tess McCabe www.tessmccabe.com.au
Cartoons by Heck Lindsay

contents

acknowledgments

The Positive Parenting Program for Parents of Teenagers (Teen Triple P) is an initiative of the Parenting and Family Support Centre at The University of Queensland. Teen Triple P builds on the highly successful Triple P for parents of infants, toddlers, preschool and primary school age children. It is dedicated to the many parents and teenagers who have participated in the development of the program. Many of the ideas and principles of positive parenting contained in this book have evolved as a result of the experience and feedback provided by parents and teenagers participating in research and therapy programs. Their assistance is gratefully acknowledged. The authors wish to acknowledge colleagues Carol Markie-Dadds and Karen Turner who contributed to the development of Triple P targeting parents of preadolescent children from which this present series evolved. We also acknowledge the financial support of the Australian Rotary Health Research Fund, Criminology Research Council, Australian Research Council, and the School of Psychology at The University of Queensland.

about the authors

Dr Alan Ralph is Adjunct Associate Professor of Clinical Psychology and Principal Research Fellow at The University of Queensland. Over the past 20 years, Alan has held several clinical positions, conducted research in the area of adolescent and family problems, and written numerous articles and chapters on related topics for scientific journals and publications. He has developed programs to assist teenagers and their parents to manage problems commonly encountered during the transition into adolescence and adulthood and trained many psychologists and other practitioners to implement these programs.

Dr Matthew R. Sanders is Professor of Clinical Psychology and Director of the Parenting and Family Support Centre at The University of Queensland. Over the past 30 years, Matt has gained an international reputation for scientific research into the family-based treatment and prevention of behavioural and emotional problems in children. He has written numerous articles on parent training and evidence-based family interventions for scientific journals and authored several books on the treatment of children's behaviour problems, including the popular parenting book Every Parent: A Positive Approach to Children's Behaviour.

The authors have combined their research and clinical experience to develop Teen Triple P specifically for parents of teenagers. This has involved writing parenting tip sheets and workbooks, as well as professional training programs and manuals. They also conduct skills training workshops for parents, and health, education and welfare professionals. Their hands-on assistance to families has guided the development of programs to manage common developmental issues and child and teenager behaviour problems such as disobedience, aggression, peer relationship problems, school-based difficulties, family conflict, and other everyday difficulties experienced by parents and teenagers.

introduction

The Positive Parenting Program for parents of teenagers (Teen Triple P) aims to make parenting easier. This workbook offers suggestions and ideas on positive parenting to help you promote your teenager's development.

Many parents approach the prospect of their children becoming teenagers with some apprehension and the teenage years certainly bring many challenges for all concerned. Teenagers have to cope with many physical changes to their bodies as they go through puberty. Sexual maturation occurs at different times and this can make them very self-conscious and sensitive to comments. The move into high school brings increasing demands for independence and responsibility. Teenagers are expected to make more decisions for themselves. This includes being more self-directed with schoolwork, and developing their own beliefs about who they are and what they want to do with their lives. They are also exposed to a range of widely differing and conflicting views and opinions from peers, teachers, parents, and the media. Sometimes teenagers may be tempted to experiment in ways that might put their health or future prospects at risk. Some risk-taking is normal and short-lived, but it can be very worrying for parents who need to monitor teenagers' behaviour closely and take action when necessary to prevent serious or long-term risk-taking.

The challenge for parents is to provide a home environment that guides and supports teenagers as they strive to become independent, well-adjusted young adults. This will often mean finding ways to deal with conflicts that may occur when the views and wishes of parents and teenagers differ. The effort required, though sometimes difficult, can lead to a close rewarding friendship between parent and teenager.

There is no single right way to be a parent and there are many different views on how parents should go about raising a teenager. Ultimately, you as the parent need to develop your own approach to dealing with your teenager's behaviour. Teen Triple P has been helpful for many parents and may give you some useful ideas to help you meet the challenges of raising teenagers.

Creating and maintaining good family relationships takes time and effort. You will probably discover that you already use some of the ideas and suggestions in this workbook. We hope you will also find some new ideas that will help improve the relationship between you and your teenager/s. You might like to complete the Issues Checklist when you get to it on page 14. This will give you an idea of the areas where there is room for improvement as you begin the program.

how to use this workbook

This workbook can be used alone or in conjunction with other Teen Triple P resources. Each week you will be encouraged to read sections of your workbook and complete several associated exercises. You may also have the opportunity to watch segments of Every Parent's Guide to Teenagers, a DVD that provides a general overview of positive approaches to parenting with step-by-step explanations and demonstrations of a variety of parenting strategies.

Self-Help Teen Triple P has been designed to make sure you have the necessary information and skills needed to practise the positive parenting strategies as soon as possible. This means you may find that some weeks have a larger amount of reading and perhaps a few more exercises to complete than other weeks. The exercises have been designed to help you use suggested strategies with your own family. Each week, you will be asked to practise some of the skills introduced in the workbook. This is to give you an opportunity to try out the suggested ideas. You may be tempted to miss some of the exercises. However, each exercise has been designed to help you get the most out of the program and it is important that you make a commitment to doing as many as you can.

You will find that spending the extra minute or two to note down your ideas in the spaces provided really helps you to be clearer about what you want to change. You will also be encouraged to set achievable goals, and to record progress toward these goals. Some weeks will include structured tasks that will help you to reach your goals. While some of these may seem unusual, many parents find them very helpful, and you will be shown how to phase them out at the end of the program.

The program has been designed to take between 7 and 10 weeks to complete. In two-parent families, it is recommended that both parents complete this program if possible.

Teen Triple P resource materials

Teen Triple P tip sheet series

The booklet Positive Parenting for Parents with Teenagers is the first in a series of parenting tip sheets designed to give parents practical information and advice on positive approaches to parenting teenagers. The ideas in this booklet can be used to promote healthy development in teenagers and to deal with a wide variety of common behavioural and emotional difficulties. The individual tip sheets in the Teen Triple P series will be most useful if you first become familiar with the ideas in the positive parenting booklet or Teen Triple P Self-Help Workbook. After reading this material, refer to the individual tip sheets for help with specific topics. There are other booklets and tip sheets for infants, toddlers, preschoolers, primary schoolers, and general parenting issues.

every parent dvd series

You may also find it useful to view a companion DVD, *Every Parent's Guide to Teenagers* which illustrates each positive parenting strategy.

Other DVDs in the series are:

- *Every Parent's Survival Guide*
- *Every Parent's Guide to Infants and Toddlers*
- *Every Parent's Guide to Preschoolers*
- *Every Parent's Guide to Primary Schoolers*

where to find these resources

For more information and to order these resources, visit the Triple P website at www.triplep.net. Alternatively phone (07) 3236 1212 if calling from within Australia or 61 7 3236 1212 if calling internationally. Ask for the Teen Triple P tip sheets and Every Parent DVD series at your local school, general practitioner, community health centre or library.

your commitment

This program is designed to support you in your parenting role. It will require your commitment, your time and your full participation if it is to achieve its aim. If you work through the program, you will be rewarded with improved family relationships. As you begin reading and completing the exercises that follow, you will learn new skills and possibly new ways of thinking, acting and organising your life. If you practise these new skills and keep up your level of motivation, the program will be of more benefit to you. So, before beginning, carefully consider your level of commitment or determination to complete this program. Below you will find a declaration of intent to complete for yourself and your partner (if appropriate). This declaration is simply an agreement you make with yourself to see the program through to completion.

Parent one

I (name) .... agree to play an active role throughout the program. I am able to: (please tick the boxes corresponding to the aspects of the program you are able to take part in)

☐ set aside 1 hour or more a week to work through the program

☐ complete the readings and exercises

☐ complete the practice tasks suggested

Signed: .... Date: ....

Witness: ....

Parent two (if appropriate)

I (name) .... agree to play an active role throughout the program. I am able to: (please tick the boxes corresponding to the aspects of the program you are able to take part in)

☐ set aside 1 hour or more a week to work through the program

☐ complete the readings and exercises

☐ complete the practice tasks suggested

Signed: .... Date: ....

Witness: ....

Now that you have decided to participate, we wish you well and hope that you find the program helpful and informative.

overview of self-help Teen Triple P

WEEK	TOPICS COVERED
1.	• what is positive parenting? • factors influencing teenagers' behaviour • goals for change • keeping track of teenagers' behaviour
2.	• developing positive relationships with teenagers • increasing desirable behaviour • teaching new skills and behaviours • using behaviour contracts • holding family meetings
3.	• managing problem behaviour • dealing with emotional behaviour • using behaviour contracts
4.	• setting goals for practice • monitoring your implementation of strategies • reviewing your use of the strategies • selecting tasks for the next week
5.	• setting goals for practice (optional) • monitoring your implementation of strategies • reviewing your use of the strategies • selecting tasks for the next week
6.	• setting goals for practice (optional) • monitoring your implementation of strategies • reviewing your use of the strategies • selecting tasks for the next week
7.	• identifying risky situations • routine for dealing with risky behaviour • family survival tips
8.	• reviewing your use of the routine for dealing with risky behaviour • reviewing your use of the strategies • selecting tasks for the next week
9.	• reviewing your use of the routine for dealing with risky behaviour (optional) • reviewing your use of the strategies • selecting tasks for the next week
10.	• reviewing your use of the routine for dealing with risky behaviour • phasing out the program • update on progress • maintaining changes • future goals

a few survival tips

All parents raising teenagers find it easier when they get support. Raising teenagers can be challenging and this task can be made less stressful if parents don't have to do it on their own.

Where there are two parents involved, discuss issues with each other, agree on discipline procedures, and support and back up each other's parenting efforts. If you have disagreements, try to deal with them when your teenager is not present, or at least reach some agreement rather than leaving it unresolved.

Other supports can be provided by family, friends, neighbours, and the parents of other teenagers. Talk about your experiences and share ideas. If you can, build up a network of the parents of your teenager's friends. This will help you to monitor what they are doing and who they are with, and to compare notes on current events.

Finally, make sure you spend time on meeting your own needs. Everyone needs to be able to get a break from parenting from time to time. Parents who find the time to do things they enjoy usually find it easier to help meet the needs of their children and teenagers.

positive parenting

overview

During Week 1 you will be introduced to the aims of Teen Triple P and what the program involves. There will be an opportunity for you to think about some of your experiences and ideas about being a parent. You will be introduced to positive parenting as an approach to raising teenagers. You will then look at factors that influence teenagers' behaviour, set goals for change and start to keep track of your teenager's behaviour.

By the end of Week 1 you should be able to:

- Describe positive parenting and what it involves.
- Identify factors that play a role in your teenager's behaviour patterns.
- Set goals for change in your teenager's and your own behaviour.
- Start monitoring one or two of your teenager's behaviours.

reasons for completing self-help Teen Triple P

Think about why you are participating in Self-Help Teen Triple P. You may hope to get some suggestions on how to cope with challenging teenager behaviour such as aggression, disobedience, rudeness and disrespect. You may be looking for solutions to some every day parenting concerns such as getting your teenage children to take responsibility for getting to school, helping around the house, speaking politely or keeping their room tidy. You may simply be interested in finding out about positive parenting strategies for promoting your teenager's development or avoiding risky situations.

▪ exercise 1 what you would like to get out of the program

Note down in the space below what you hope to get from completing Self-Help Teen Triple P.

....

....

....

....

....

....

....

Whatever your reasons for taking part in the program, we congratulate you for coming this far and hope that both you and your teenager benefit from the program in very practical ways.

what is positive parenting?

Positive parenting is an approach to parenting that aims to help you promote teenagers' development and manage teenagers' behaviour in a constructive and non-hurtful way. It is based on good communication and positive attention to help teenagers develop the skills they need to become mature adults. Teenagers who grow up with positive parenting are likely to develop appropriate skills and feel good about themselves. They are also less likely to develop behaviour problems. There are five key aspects to positive parenting.

ensuring a safe, engaging environment

Your teenager needs a safe but stimulating environment. As children grow older, they need to learn how to safely take on more responsibility around the home. This will include knowing how to operate gas and electrical appliances, use fire extinguishers and give basic first aid, and being competent when using power tools such as drills, saws, and mowers.

Parents also need to encourage teenagers to become involved in organised, meaningful activities at school and elsewhere, where there is appropriate adult supervision and monitoring. Appropriate supervision and monitoring of teenagers really means knowing where they are, who they are with, and what they are doing, especially when they are away from home.

creating a positive learning environment

Older children and teenagers need to feel valued as they strive to take on adult roles and responsibilities. The best way to promote this is by gradually increasing their involvement in family decision-making. Issues will range from the relatively trivial (what name to give the new pet), to the more important (what high school to attend). Parents will still usually have the final word on many issues, especially where there may be considerable risk. Encouraging teenagers to regularly participate in discussing family issues ensures they will become skilled at making good personal decisions.

Parents need to be available to teenagers, just like when they were younger. Teenagers may have different needs and problems, but attention and encouragement are still powerful ways of signaling your approval and pleasure. When you see your teenager doing something you like, make sure you let them know. This should make it more likely they will do it again.

using assertive discipline

When children are younger, parents tend to decide what behaviour is appropriate, and what will happen when misbehaviour occurs. As children grow into their teenage years, it is important to involve them in negotiating what the rules and responsibilities might be, and what privileges they can expect to enjoy in return.

Negotiation involves you and your teenager jointly discussing and deciding what responsibilities go with being a part of your family, and what privileges may be allowed if those responsibilities are met. This often requires compromise, trying out new arrangements, and monitoring progress. Spelling out in advance what behaviour is expected, as well as the consequences for unacceptable behaviour, can reduce conflict by helping everyone to keep calm when unacceptable teenage behaviour occurs.

having realistic expectations

Parents' expectations of their teenagers depend on what they consider appropriate behaviour at different ages. No two teenagers are the same, and although individual differences will have generally shown up by now, additional changes in development may become noticeable during the early teenage years. The onset of puberty may affect behaviour in different ways, and peer pressure may become a major issue. It is important that you talk to other parents whenever possible to find out whether they are experiencing similar problems. Teenagers will push the limits set by parents as they see some of their peers enjoying greater apparent freedom. It is important to be realistic about the risks associated with increased teenage freedom, and ensure your teenager learns how to deal with temptations that may lead to undesirable consequences. It is also important for parents to have realistic expectations of themselves. It is fine to want to be a good parent, but to aim to be a perfect parent is setting yourself up for disappointment, for frustration, and for experiencing lots of hassles with your teenager. So be realistic. Every parent makes mistakes. Most mistakes are minor, and parents have to learn as they go.

taking care of yourself as a parent

Parenting is easier when personal needs for intimacy, companionship, recreation and time alone are being met. Being a good parent does not mean that your teenager should dominate your life. If your own needs as an adult are being met, it is much easier to be patient, consistent and available to your teenager. In the space below, list those changes that you would like to see in your teenager's behaviour and your own behaviour. Make sure your goals are specific and achievable and worded positively if possible.

■ exercise 2 what is positive parenting?

Which of these positive parenting skills do you find easy? Why?

....

....

....

....

Which do you find difficult? Why?

....

....

....

....

What other things are important in helping teenagers develop?

....

....

....

....

factors influencing teenagers' behaviour

Why do teenagers behave as they do? How is it that teenagers from the same family can be so alike in some ways and so different in others? To understand how teenagers' behaviour develops, we need to consider three things – their genetic make-up, their family environment, and the community in which they live. These factors interact to shape the skills, attitudes and abilities teenagers develop, and also influence whether they develop behaviour problems.

exercise 3 identifying factors influencing teenagers' behaviour

Teenagers behave in both desirable and undesirable ways for a reason.

By understanding these reasons we can look at what changes we need to make in both our teenager's and our own behaviour to prevent behaviour problems. In this exercise, the aim is for you to get an understanding of what might be going on in your family that could influence your teenager's behaviour. Since you know your teenager better than anyone else, you are the expert. The following section presents some possible influences on teenagers' behaviour. As you read through it, ask yourself three questions: *Does this apply to my teenager? Which factors could be most important in explaining my teenager's behaviour? Is there anything else I think is important that is not on the list?* If possible, watch the segment of the DVD *Every Parent's Guide to Teenagers* that covers this material. There is space in your workbook to place a mark next to those factors that you think play a role in shaping your teenager's behaviour.

You may also like to add some comments of your own.

For two-parent families, it is important for each parent to focus on themselves rather than on their partner. Avoid blaming your partner for your teenager's behaviour. Try to focus on your own parenting styles.

genetic make-up

Children inherit a unique genetic make-up from their parents. This may include physical characteristics, such as eye colour and hair texture, as well as some behavioural and emotional characteristics. For example, teenagers who have problems concentrating, or who have a tendency to feel sad or depressed may have inherited a genetic make-up that makes them more likely to have these problems.

Children may also inherit their temperament from their parents, such as how sociable or outgoing they are, how active they are, or how emotional they are. Some of these characteristics can make teenagers difficult to manage. Some of these characteristics can be quite stable throughout life, while some seem to change and are replaced by others, particularly after puberty. While these factors can contribute to a teenager's problem behaviour, the way other people respond to that behaviour can also be very important.

What was your teenager like when they were younger?

- demanded lots of attention ☐
- emotional and difficult to manage ☐
- very active, always on the go ☐
- quiet and withdrawn ☐

Comments:

....

....

....

....

the family environment

A person's genetic make-up is something that cannot be changed. However, children learn a lot from their family environment, and this can be changed to teach them to behave in a more appropriate way. The effects of family environment on children's behaviour are best thought of as being like gusts of wind. Each gust has a very small effect, pushing the child only slightly in a certain direction, but over time, if the wind is constant, large effects can be seen. Understanding how children learn from their environment is extremely useful in deciding how to avoid serious problems, and reduce conflict when it occurs.

Do any of these accidental rewards occur in your family?

- social attention ☐
- material rewards ☐
- activity rewards ☐
- avoiding chores ☐

Comments:

....

....

....

....

accidental rewards for misbehaviour

Teenagers can sometimes get what they want by behaving in ways that parents don't like. Problem behaviour is likely to keep occurring if it results in accidental rewards. Sometimes parents may not realise this is happening. For example, if you accidentally laugh or spend a lot of time reasoning with your teenager the first time they say a swear word, the extra attention may encourage your teenager to swear again. A teenager may discover that if they complain of feeling unwell, they get a lot of sympathetic attention and can perhaps also avoid doing unpleasant activities, such as homework. A gradual increase in complaining about feeling unwell may be the result. Accidental rewards can include social attention (such as talking or laughing), material rewards (such as money or things they want), activities (such as being driven somewhere or having a friend over), or avoiding chores (such as getting out of doing homework or washing the dishes).

escalation traps

Teenagers may learn that 'turning up' or escalating undesirable behaviour is effective in getting what they want when their first request is turned down. For example, a teenager who wants to stay up late and watch a particular movie on TV may gradually become more aggressive, and complain loudly and emotionally of your unfair behaviour. After several minutes of this, you may give in and allow them to watch the movie. The persistent and escalating demands by the teenager are rewarded by getting what they want. This increases the chances such demands will happen again in similar circumstances. In addition, your giving in is also rewarded by your teenager stopping their demands. This increases the chances that you will give in sooner next time.

Parents can also learn that if they escalate and get louder when they want their teenager to do something, their teenager is more likely to eventually comply with their requests. For example, you make a request for the TV to be turned off — your teenager ignores you! You repeat the request more loudly — still no result. Finally, you angrily demand that the TV be turned off before you count to 3 — or else! Your teenager finally complies, having learned that they only have to take notice of you when you count and threaten. Your escalating yelling and threatening are rewarded by the TV eventually being turned off, and this increases the chances you will yell and threaten more quickly in the future. The teenager's delaying tactics are also rewarded by getting to watch a bit more TV, and then avoiding the threatened consequences by complying just before you explode. If this pattern of behaviour has been a feature of your family for some time, it may now be quite serious, with loud disputes between you and your teenager. As children grow older, they push the limits more. As they become bigger, stronger, and more verbally skilled, louder and longer fights are likely. In some families, parents become worn down by such persistent behaviour and end up giving in without making any attempt to negotiate a reasonable outcome.

Do either of these escalation traps occur in your family?

- teenager escalates ☐
- parent escalates ☐

Comments:

....

....

....

....

ignoring desirable behaviour

For some teenagers there is little or no payoff for good behaviour. Despite what some parents may believe, their attention is very important to teenagers. Behaviour that earns no attention is likely to happen less often and may even stop altogether. If teenagers are ignored when they behave well, they may learn that the only way to get attention is to misbehave. As children grow older, they also learn that other people will give them attention — their peers. Sometimes behaviour that parents find desirable will be increased by peers (such as improving at sport), but often peer approval will increase behaviour that parents do not find desirable (such as body piercing).

Do you often fall into this trap?

• ignoring desirable behaviour ☐

Comments:

....

....

....

....

watching others

Teenagers learn a lot by watching what other people do, particularly their parents. For example, when parents get angry and yell, and get their own way because they yell, teenagers learn that it is acceptable to yell when they have a problem. Teenagers whose parents often hit them are likely to hit a lot as well. Behaviours such as yelling, talking back, losing your temper, swearing, hitting, and how to react when something frightening happens, can all be learned through watching others. Teenagers may also directly challenge parents who ask for a change of behaviour, stating *You do it, why shouldn't I?*

Does your teenager pick up any bad habits from watching others at home?

• parents ☐

• siblings ☐

Comments:

....

....

....

....

making requests

The way that parents attempt to get their teenagers to do things can influence whether or not they will cooperate. With younger children, parents often feel responsible for getting them to do things, like brush their teeth, eat their breakfast, wash their hands. However, older children and teenagers should be taking on these responsibilities without parents having to nag them constantly. Some common problems include:

• *Not enough information.* Teenagers sometimes seem disobedient because no-one has given them sufficient information about what is expected. Unless discussed previously, the request *Clean your room* does not specify what exactly it is that needs to be done. Does it mean − Sweep the floor? Pick up the clothes? Make the bed? Wash the windows? Or all of the above?

- *Poorly timed.* Requests made when a teenager is busy doing something else are likely to be not heard or ignored. Most of us don't like to be interrupted when we are busy and teenagers are no different.
- *Too vague.* Teenagers are unlikely (or unable) to follow requests that are unclear, such as *Stop that!* or *Don't be stupid!* Requests that appear optional and do not suggest a parent expects cooperation are also likely to be turned down, such as *Would you like to do your homework now?*

How do you make requests?

- not enough information ☐
- poorly timed ☐
- too vague ☐

Comments:

....

....

....

....

emotional messages

Parents who disapprove of their teenager rather than their teenager's behaviour may lower their teenager's self esteem. Calling a teenager names — *stupid* or *idiot* — and guilt-inducing messages — *Your mother will be so upset when she hears about this* — may shame teenagers into cooperating. However, this can make teenagers angry, resentful and uncooperative.

Do you give any of these emotional messages?

- name calling or put downs ☐
- guilt inducing messages ☐

Comments:

....

....

....

....

ineffective use of punishment

Teenagers can develop behaviour problems because of the way parents use punishment or discipline. Here are some reasons why punishment does not work.

- *Punishment not carried out.* Teenagers who have learned over the years that parents rarely carry through with punishment will call their bluff regularly.
- *Threatening to use punishment.* Threatening a teenager with punishment can increase the emotional temperature and make an argument more likely. Over time teenagers will learn to ignore any request that does not include a threat. Sometimes teenagers will treat a threat as a dare and will test it to see what happens.
- *Punishment given in anger.* With young children, there is always a risk of losing control and injuring the child. With older children and teenagers, everyone can get injured, sometimes seriously.
- *Delayed punishment.* Sometimes parents overreact to problem behaviour because they wait until the behaviour is intolerable before doing something about it. With teenagers, this will often result in everyone yelling and losing their temper, and then not speaking to each other for days afterwards.
- *Inconsistent use of punishment.* Inconsistency makes it difficult for teenagers to learn what is expected of them. Punishing a behaviour on one occasion, and ignoring it the next time sends a confusing message. Problems can also arise when parents contradict or undermine each other, or do not back each other up. Teenagers will learn which parent to approach for particular requests, and this can cause relationship problems between parents.

Do you have any of these difficulties with discipline?

- punishment not carried out ☐
- threatening to use punishment ☐
- punishment given in anger ☐
- delayed punishment ☐
- inconsistent use of punishment ☐

Comments:

....

....

....

....

parents' beliefs and expectations

Some beliefs are unhelpful and can make parenting difficult. Here are some common unhelpful beliefs.

- *It's just a phase.* This belief can stop parents from dealing with problem behaviour straight away. Instead, parents may wait until a problem is severe and long standing before seeking help or making changes.
- *They ought to know better.* Wishful thinking about how teenagers 'ought' to behave rarely results in improvement. Maybe the rules are not clear or perhaps there are other consequences competing with parental approval.

- *They're doing it deliberately, just to annoy me.* This belief places blame on the teenager and may make parents resentful, leading them to overreact to misbehaviour. It may also stop parents from looking at how their own actions contribute to the problem behaviour.
- *It's all my fault they're the way they are.* This belief blames parents for teenagers' problem behaviour. Parents may feel guilty and depressed if they think they are to blame for their teenager's behaviour. This makes it even harder to be patient, calm and consistent with their teenager.

Parents' expectations can also make parenting more difficult. It is unrealistic for parents to expect their teenager to be perfect. This is likely to lead to disappointment and conflict with their teenager. Parents can also have unrealistic expectations of themselves. When parents aim to do a perfect job, they are setting themselves up for dissatisfaction and frustration.

Do any of these apply to you?

- unhelpful beliefs ☐
- unrealistic expectations ☐

Comments:

....

....

....

....

other influences on the family

There are other influences on parents' wellbeing that can make parenting more difficult. Here are some examples:

- *Parents' relationship.* Problem behaviour can occur when a couple's relationship is strained and there is tension and conflict in the home. Boys may become aggressive and girls may become anxious or depressed when they see a lot of arguments and fights between their parents.
- *Parents' emotions.* Parents' feelings, such as anger, depression or anxiety, can prevent them from being consistent and managing their teenager's behaviour effectively. For example, if a parent is feeling sad or depressed, they are likely to be irritable and impatient, have unhelpful thoughts about their teenager, want to spend less time with their teenager, and provide less supervision.
- *Stress.* All parents experience stress at some time, such as moving house, financial problems, and work pressures. Teenagers need routine and may become upset if these stresses disrupt the usual family routine for a long period of time.

Do any of these apply to your family?

- parents' relationship with each other ☐
- parents' feelings ☐
- stress ☐

Comments:

....

....

....

....

influences outside the home

Teenagers' behaviour is also influenced by factors outside the home, once they have more contact with others in the community.

peers and friends

As teenagers mix more with other teenagers at school and in social groups, they will be influenced by their relationships with these peers. For example, aggressive and disruptive children often fail to develop good social skills and may be rejected by many of their peers. They are then likely to mix with and learn from other disruptive teenagers. If this trend continues through the teenage years, it is likely that this will disrupt their schooling, and possibly bring them into contact with police and corrective services.

school

Experiences at school can influence teenagers' adjustment and behaviour. For example if early problems are not identified and addressed, this may lead to academic failure, dislike of school, early dropout, and poor job prospects.

media and technology

The influence of the media and computer technologies is a major factor for many teenagers. It is almost impossible for parents to control all access to movies, magazines, radio, TV, computer games, and websites. Problem behaviour such as swearing, fighting, smoking, drinking, and engaging in inappropriate sexual activity can be learned from these sources.

Are you concerned about any of these community influences on your teenager's behaviour?

- peers and friends ☐
- school ☐
- media and technology ☐

Comments:

....

....

....

....

All parents can fall into parenting traps at times. You would probably need to be superhuman to raise your teenager without ever giving an accidental reward or falling into an escalation trap or being inconsistent. Really it is not possible to be a parent without making some mistakes along the way. However, teenager behaviour problems are more likely to occur if you find you are often falling into these parenting traps. So, how often these day to day interactions occur is far more important than simply whether or not they occur.

goals for change

Now that you have looked at the possible factors influencing teenagers' behaviour, think about changes you would like to see in your teenager's behaviour, as well as in your own. It is up to you, the parent, to decide what skills to teach your teenager. It may be helpful to have in mind the skills that help teenagers learn to be independent and to get along with others.

■ exercise 4 what skills should we encourage in teenagers?

Look at the list below and think about skills you would like to encourage in your teenager. Pick two or three that are important for you and your teenager.

How to communicate and get on with others

- expressing their views, ideas and needs appropriately
- requesting assistance or help when they need it
- cooperating with adult requests
- interacting cooperatively with others in an age-appropriate way
- being aware of the feelings of others
- being aware of how their own actions affect others

How to manage their feelings

- expressing feelings in ways that do not harm others
- controlling hurtful actions and thinking before acting
- developing positive feelings about themselves and others
- accepting rules and limits

How to be independent

- doing things for themselves
- completing tasks without constant adult supervision
- being responsible for their own actions

How to solve problems

- showing an interest in everyday things
- asking questions and developing ideas
- considering alternative solutions to problems
- negotiating and compromising
- making decisions and accepting the consequences of those decisions

Comments:

....

....

....

....

■ exercise 5 setting goals for change

It is now time to start thinking about goals for change. It is important to set goals at the start of Self-Help Teen Triple P. This way you will know what you are working towards and whether you are making progress. When developing your goals for change, consider your teenager's behaviour now. Think of what you would like your teenager to do more often (e.g. speak politely, complete chores without constant reminding, cooperate with your requests, let you know where they are). Also consider what you would like your teenager to do less often (e.g. argue, fight, complain, interrupt, take things without asking).

To assist in setting goals for change, you may wish to complete the Issues Checklist below. It will also give you a measure of how you and your teenager are getting on in relation to many of the common issues that cause conflict in families. The checklist contains a list of things that sometimes get talked about at home. Circle Yes for the topics that you and your teenager have talked about at all during the last 4 weeks. Circle No for those topics that have not come up. Then where you have circled yes, circle the number on the right that best matches how hot your discussions on each topic have been. If both parents wish to complete the Checklist, either use different coloured pens, or use the spare copy in the Worksheets section at the end of the workbook.

issues checklist

Topic	Yes/No		Calm	A little angry			Angry
1. telephone calls	yes	no	1	2	3	4	5
2. time for going to bed	yes	no	1	2	3	4	5
3. cleaning up bedroom	yes	no	1	2	3	4	5
4. doing homework	yes	no	1	2	3	4	5
5. putting away clothes	yes	no	1	2	3	4	5
6. using the television or computer	yes	no	1	2	3	4	5
7. cleanliness (washing, showers, teeth)	yes	no	1	2	3	4	5

Topic	Yes/No		Calm	A little angry			Angry
8. which clothes to wear	yes	no	1	2	3	4	5
9. how neat clothing looks	yes	no	1	2	3	4	5
10. making too much noise at home	yes	no	1	2	3	4	5
11. table manners	yes	no	1	2	3	4	5
12. fighting with brothers or sisters	yes	no	1	2	3	4	5
13. swearing or bad language	yes	no	1	2	3	4	5
14. how money is spent	yes	no	1	2	3	4	5
15. picking books or movies	yes	no	1	2	3	4	5
16. allowance/pocket money	yes	no	1	2	3	4	5
17. going places without parents (shopping, movies, etc.)	yes	no	1	2	3	4	5
18. playing music too loudly	yes	no	1	2	3	4	5
19. turning things off in the house (e.g. lights, TV, computer)	yes	no	1	2	3	4	5
20. drugs	yes	no	1	2	3	4	5
21. taking care of things (e.g. CDs, books, games, bikes, pets, etc.)	yes	no	1	2	3	4	5
22. drinking beer, wine, or other alcohol	yes	no	1	2	3	4	5
23. buying CDs, books, games, magazines	yes	no	1	2	3	4	5
24. going on dates	yes	no	1	2	3	4	5
25. who they should be friends with	yes	no	1	2	3	4	5
26. selecting new clothes	yes	no	1	2	3	4	5
27. sex	yes	no	1	2	3	4	5
28. coming home on time	yes	no	1	2	3	4	5
29. getting to school on time	yes	no	1	2	3	4	5
30. getting low grades in school	yes	no	1	2	3	4	5
31. getting in trouble in school	yes	no	1	2	3	4	5
32. lying	yes	no	1	2	3	4	5
33. helping out around the home	yes	no	1	2	3	4	5
34. talking back to parents	yes	no	1	2	3	4	5
35. getting up in the morning	yes	no	1	2	3	4	5
36. bothering parents when they want to be left alone	yes	no	1	2	3	4	5
37. bothering teenager when he or she wants to be left alone	yes	no	1	2	3	4	5
38. putting feet on furniture	yes	no	1	2	3	4	5
39. messing up the house	yes	no	1	2	3	4	5
40. what time to have meals	yes	no	1	2	3	4	5
41. how to spend free time	yes	no	1	2	3	4	5
42. smoking	yes	no	1	2	3	4	5
43. earning money away from home	yes	no	1	2	3	4	5
44. what teenager eats	yes	no	1	2	3	4	5

To score your responses, first simply add up the number of times you circled **yes**. This should be a number between 0 and 44. Write your score here.

A

Next, add up all the numbers you circled on the right. This should be a number between 0 and 220. Write this score here.

B

Finally, divide the number in the lower box (B) by the number in the higher box (A). This will give you the average intensity of the discussions you had with your teenager. Write the answer here.

For example, if you circled yes 30 times (box A), and your intensity scores (box B) totaled 120, your average intensity score will be 120/30 = 4. This means that on a scale of 1 to 5, many of your discussions with your teenager appear to be quite heated and you may wish to set a goal to have calmer discussions. You can also use the Checklist to identify specific issues where you want your teenager to improve, such as cleaning up their bedroom, helping around the house, or being more polite when they speak to you.

Generally speaking, if you have scored yes more than 25 times, this suggests that you are experiencing more difficulty with your teenager than most parents do. Also, if your average intensity score (between 1 and 5) is higher than 2.2, this suggests that your discussions with your teenager are more angry than most parents experience. You may find it useful to compare these scores with your scores when you repeat the Issues Checklist at the end of the program.

The Issues Checklist is reproduced with the permission of Dr. Ronald J. Prinz

Now that you have had the opportunity to think about what changes you would like to see, write your goals for your teenager in the left-hand column below. It is also important to consider what changes you would like to make to your own behaviour. Now that you have looked at what may contribute to your teenager's problem behaviour, you may like to set yourself some goals too. Consider what you would like to do more often (e.g. stay calm, make clear requests) and what you would like to do less often (e.g. use threats, shout instructions from a distance). Write the goals for your own behaviour in the right-hand column.

In the space below, list those changes that you would like to see in your teenager's behaviour and your own behaviour. Make sure your goals are specific and achievable and worded positively if possible.

GOALS FOR CHANGE IN YOUR TEENAGER'S BEHAVIOUR	GOALS FOR CHANGE IN YOUR OWN BEHAVIOUR

keeping track of teenagers' behaviour

To help you know how close you are getting to achieving your goals, it is useful to keep track of your teenager's and your own behaviour. Keeping a record is helpful for many reasons:

- It gives you a chance to check out whether what you think about your teenager's behaviour is actually true.
- It helps you see your own reactions to your teenager's behaviour and identify when and why the behaviour occurs.
- It allows you to see whether the behaviour is improving, worsening, or staying the same.
- It tells you when you have achieved your goal.

Several monitoring forms are available to help you keep track of behaviour. This next section describes some ways of keeping track of behaviour, and there is also a segment on the DVD *Every Parent's Guide to Teenagers*.

behaviour diary

If you are concerned about some aspect of your teenager's behaviour, it is useful to keep track by keeping a behaviour diary. This involves writing down when and where a problem behaviour occurred, what happened before the problem behaviour (what led up to it) and what happened afterwards (how you reacted). This will help you to identify:

- patterns in your teenager's behaviour
- how consistently you deal with your teenager's behaviour
- high-risk times or situations
- possible triggers or causes
- possible accidental rewards

Use this form for behaviours that occur less than five times per day. For behaviours that occur more often, choose another recording form. Even if you choose another form, you may like to also use this form for one or two examples each day of a behaviour that occurs often. An example behaviour diary is shown on the next page.

example behaviour diary

Problem behaviour: Peter's angry yelling

Day: Friday

PROBLEM	WHEN AND WHERE DID IT HAPPEN?	WHAT HAPPENED BEFORE?	WHAT HAPPENED AFTER?	OTHER COMMENTS
Shouting at sister	7.30 a.m. Near bathroom	Sister using bathroom	Sister shouted back, dad sorted it out	Rushing to get ready for school
Angry at mother	8.00 a.m. Kitchen	Packing lunch in school bag	Got extra money for snacks	Didn't like lunch mother provided
Yelling at mother	4.00 p.m. Family room	Told to do homework before going out to see friends	Went out to see friends anyway	Couldn't be bothered arguing with him
Angry at sister	6.00 p.m. Kitchen	Sister using sink to wash dishes	Pushed in to get a drink of water from tap	Too tired to interfere
Angry at father	7.30 p.m. Family room	Father came home without magazine	Peter and father yelled at each other. Peter sent to his room	Father had promised to buy magazine for Peter and forgot

tally sheet

Another way to keep track of your teenager's behaviour is to write down how often something occurs. To do this, use a tally sheet like the one below, and mark off each time the behaviour occurs during the day. Use this form for behaviours that occur no more than 15 times per day. For behaviours that occur more often choose another recording form.

example tally sheet

Instructions: Write the day in the first column, then place a tick in the next column each time the behaviour happens on that day. Record the total number of ticks for each day in the end column.

Behaviour: Swearing

Start date: Sunday 11 May

DAY	1	2	3	4	5	6	7	8	9	10	11	12	13	14	15	TOTAL
Sun	✓	✓	✓	✓	✓	✓	✓	✓	✓							9
Mon	✓	✓	✓	✓	✓	✓	✓	✓	✓	✓	✓					11
Tues	✓	✓	✓	✓	✓	✓	✓	✓								8

duration record

Sometimes the number of times a behaviour occurs is not the crucial issue. It may be more important to note the duration of a behaviour. The duration record is a useful form for tracking how long a behaviour lasts, such as how long a teenager spends on the telephone, getting ready for school in the morning, or completing homework. The aim is to time how long each instance of the target behaviour lasts in minutes or hours, and write this on the chart. There may be only one instance of the behaviour per day, or there may be several. If there are several instances, at the end of the day, all episodes are added together to see the total amount of time the behaviour lasted for that day. An example duration record is included below.

Use this form when you want to know how long a behaviour lasts. For behaviours that come and go quickly or often, use a time-sampling record (see next page). Otherwise use a behaviour diary or tally sheet.

example duration record

Instructions: Write the day in the first column, then for each separate occurence of the target behaviour, record how long it lasted in seconds, minutes or hours. Total the times at the end of each day.

Behaviour: Time spent doing homework   Start Date: 20th March

DAY	SUCCESSIVE EPISODES										TOTAL
	1	2	3	4	5	6	7	8	9	10	
Tues	5 min	15 min	10 min								30 min
Wed	10 min	10 min	5 min	5 min	20 min						50 min
Thurs	15 min	5 min									20 min

time-sampling record

This form is useful when tracking behaviours that occur more than several times an hour, such as swearing, complaining or disobedience. It is best to pick a high-risk time of the day to complete this form. Choose a time period when the target behaviour is more likely to occur, such as in the morning before school, or in the late afternoon. Once you have identified a high-risk time, break this period into smaller blocks of 10, 15 or 30 minutes. Then simply put a tick in the box if the problem behaviour occurs at all during that time block. There is no need to count how many times the behaviour occurs, just tick once if it occurs at all in the time interval.

Use this form for behaviours that occur often (more than 15 times per day), behaviours that come and go quickly or often over a short period of time, or behaviours that do not have a clear beginning and end. Choose another recording form for behaviours that occur less often or are easy to monitor.

example time-sampling record

Instructions: Place a tick in the square for the corresponding time period if the target behaviour has occurred at least once.

Behaviour: Arguing or talking back

Starting Date: March 20th

TIME OF DAY	M	T	W	T	F	S	S
8.00–8.15	✓		✓	✓	✓		
8.15–8.30		✓	✓				
8.30–8.45	✓	✓	✓				
8.45–9.00					✓		
3.30–3.45			✓				✓
3.45–4.00	✓	✓	✓				
4.00–4.15	✓	✓	✓		✓		
4.15–4.30		✓	✓				
6.00–6.15	✓		✓	✓			
6.15–6.30	✓	✓	✓				
6.30–6.45	✓	✓			✓		
6.45–7.00		✓			✓		
Total	7	6	8	2	5	0	1

behaviour graph

You can also put the information on a graph to make it easier to keep track of your teenager's progress (see below). On the left, in the area headed "BASELINE", keep track like this for a week or so before you start any new parenting plan. Then, on the right continue to keep track of your teenager's behaviour after you start, to see whether your new plan is working. This will help you notice improvements in your teenager's behaviour and keep you motivated to continue using new strategies or routines.

example behaviour graph

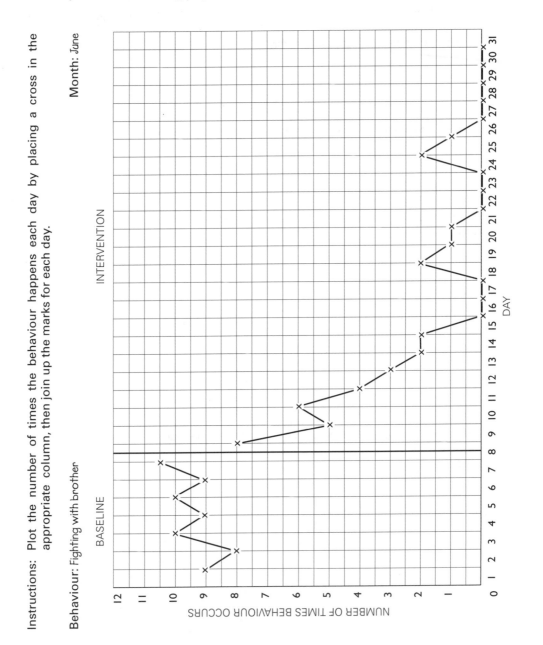

When you start a new parenting plan, it is useful to have a trial period of around 7 to 10 days. At the end of the trial period, you can decide whether to keep going in the same way or make changes to your plan. Remember, the best way to change teenagers' behaviour, and your own, is to do it gradually. Once new routines or behaviours are well established you can keep track less often, such as once a week instead of daily. Stop recording completely when you are confident of your progress. If you are concerned about your progress, seek professional help.

■ exercise 6 keeping track

In order to gain some practice in selecting an appropriate form, indicate which types of form could be used to keep track of the following behaviours. Give your reason for choosing a particular form. Often more than one form would be appropriate for the behaviours listed.

How often a teenager swears at others.

....

....

How long a teenager takes to complete homework each evening.

....

....

How often a teenager fights with brothers or sisters, particularly after school or before the evening meal.

....

....

How often a teenager helps around the house.

....

....

How often a teenager answers back or uses a disrespectful tone of voice.

....

....

You may like to refer to page 163 to check your answers.

summary

During Week 1 you have looked at what positive parenting involves and some factors influencing teenagers' behaviour. You have thought about the skills and behaviours you would like to encourage in your teenager and set some goals for change. To finish, you have looked at some ways of keeping track of your teenager's behaviour.

practice tasks

• Use your list of goals on page 17 to select one or two of your teenager's problem behaviours for baseline monitoring. Keep track of these behaviours for 7 days using a monitoring form from pages 26–30 in your workbook. Additional copies of these forms can be found in the Worksheets section at the back.

• Write down the behaviour/s you plan to track for the next 7 days. Which type of monitoring form will you use?

....

....

....

....

For a review of the material covered today, you may like to watch:

• *Every Parent's Guide to Teenagers,* Part 1, Positive Parenting.

• *Every Parent's Guide to Teenagers,* Part 2, Factors Influencing Teenagers' Behaviour, Goals for Change, Keeping Track.

content of next week

During Week 2 you will look at practical strategies for:

• Building positive relationships with teenagers.
• Increasing desirable behaviour.
• Teaching teenagers new skills and behaviours.

behaviour diary

Instructions: List the problem behaviour, when and where it happened and what happened before and after.

Problem behaviour: ....

Day: ....

PROBLEM	WHEN AND WHERE DID IT HAPPEN?	WHAT HAPPENED BEFORE?	WHAT HAPPENED AFTER?	OTHER COMMENTS

tally sheet

Instructions: Write the day in the first column, then place a tick in the next column each time the behaviour occurs on that day. Record the total number of ticks for each day in the end column.

Behaviour: ....

Start Date: ....

DAY	1	2	3	4	5	6	7	8	9	10	11	12	13	14	15	TOTAL

duration record

Instructions: Write the day in the first column, then for each separate occurence of the target behaviour, record how long it lasted in seconds, minutes or hours. Total the times at the end of each day.

Behaviour: .... Start Date: ....

DAY	SUCCESSIVE EPISODES									TOTAL

time-sampling record

Instructions: Place a tick in the square for the corresponding time period if the target behaviour has occurred at least once.

Behaviour: ....

Start Date: ....

DAYS	M	T	W	T	F	S	S	M	T	W	T	F	S	S	M	T	W	T	F	S	S

TIME OF DAY

behaviour graph

Instructions: Plot the number of times the behaviour happens each day by placing a cross on the appropriate column, then join up the marks for each day.

Behaviour: ....

Month: ....

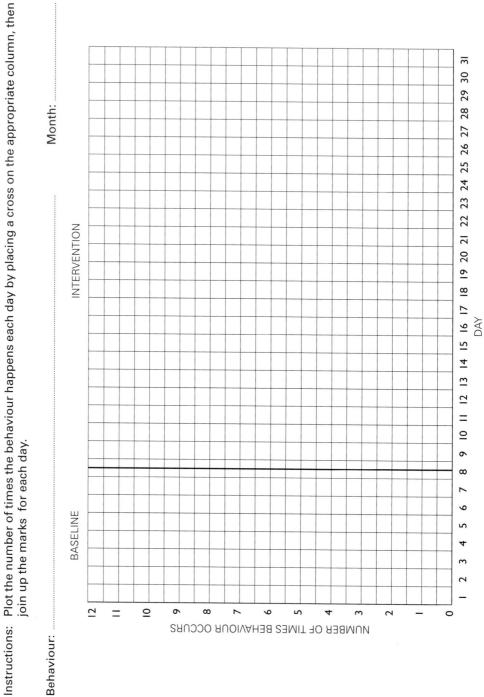

encouraging appropriate behaviour

overview

Encouragement and positive attention help teenagers develop their skills and learn appropriate ways of behaving. Encouraging the behaviour you like increases the chances of the behaviour happening again. In Week 1, you decided on some of the behaviours and skills you would like to encourage in your teenager. This week, you will be introduced to a number of strategies to try out. These strategies can help you encourage your teenager to behave appropriately by enhancing your relationship with your teenager, rewarding your teenager for desirable behaviour, and teaching your teenager new skills. As you work through the exercises, think about the strategies you would feel most comfortable using with your teenager.

By the end of Week 2 you should be able to:

- Use the strategies for developing a positive relationship with your teenager (i.e. spending time together, talking to your teenager, showing affection).
- Use the strategies for increasing desirable behaviour (i.e. descriptive praise, providing attention, and providing opportunities for engaging activities for your teenager).
- Use the strategies for teaching your teenager new skills or behaviours (i.e. setting a good example, coaching problem-solving).
- Set up a behaviour contract with appropriate rewards for your teenager.

review of progress

◼ exercise 1 review use of monitoring forms

What were your practice tasks from last week (refer to page 25)?

....

....

....

What did you find out from your monitoring? It may be helpful to look at the monitoring forms you used (see pages 26–30).

....

....

....

Is there anything that you could have done differently? You may need to continue monitoring if you missed a few days.

....

....

....

encouraging appropriate behaviour

Before looking at how to manage problem behaviour, it is important to look at how to promote your teenager's development. Many common behaviour problems can be solved or reduced by helping teenagers learn better ways of handling situations they find difficult. As you work through the exercises for this week, think about what strategies you currently use to encourage your teenager to behave appropriately. You may have heard about or already use some of these strategies, and some may be new to you. This week gives you a chance to think about your relationship with your teenager and whether you let them know when they are doing something that you like.

It is important to remember that each strategy is presented as an option for you to consider. All strategies have their limitations and no single strategy will work for all situations or in isolation. These strategies are a starting point for promoting development and encouraging appropriate behaviour, and they are intended to be used when teenagers are behaving well, rather than when they are uncooperative or misbehaving. Strategies for dealing with problem behaviour and teaching teenagers self-control will be covered next week.

developing positive relationships with teenagers

Children develop their skills best when they have a warm, predictable and secure family environment, and teenagers are no different. It takes time to form quality family relationships that last. Here are some ideas to help you develop a positive relationship with your teenager. As you work through Exercises 2 to 4, ask yourself what changes, if any, you feel you need to make to strengthen your relationship with your teenager.

spend time with your teenager

Spending frequent, small amounts of time with teenagers can be just as beneficial as less frequent longer periods. However, there will be times when longer periods are needed. Try and work out when are good times for you and your teenager. These can be when you are alone together and when there is no pressure to get things done such as driving in the car together, at bedtime, or on weekends. You may find that making small changes to your daily routine creates new opportunities to spend small amounts of time together.

■ exercise 2 ideas on how to spend time with your teenager

Write down some ideas about how you and your teenager can spend time together. Try and come up with ideas that can be used during the week and on weekends.

....

....

....

talk with your teenager

Sometimes when you are spending time together there will be an opportunity to talk. Resist the temptation to talk about things that might cause an argument.

A good way to start is with something about yourself – what happened during your day perhaps – or ask about something you know they are interested in. This might include things you have done together, or are about to do. Make sure you listen to the things your teenager talks about and show interest. Try not to slip into teaching or interrogation mode – practise asking clarifying questions, reflect what you hear them say, and occasionally offer items from your own experience. Be prepared to talk for longer if they start to talk about issues or problems. If there is not enough time, plan another time as soon as you can and keep to it.

■ exercise 3 things to talk about

List some things that interest your teenager or that you have been doing that you can talk about.

....

....

....

....

show affection

One of the best ways to maintain a good relationship with your teenager is to show them you care about them. This needs to be done differently from when they were younger, as public displays of affection may cause embarrassment – especially in front of their peers. Affection should be displayed more in keeping with adult relationships. It is important to show teenagers how to appropriately give and receive affection as an adult as this is essential in forming friendships and personal relationships.

■ exercise 4 ways to show affection

What ways of showing affection do you and your teenager both enjoy?

....

....

....

....

increasing desirable behaviour

The next challenge is how to increase those behaviours that we see occasionally but would like to see more often. Teenagers are more cooperative and less difficult to manage when they receive encouragement and positive attention for behaving well and when they have plenty of interesting and stimulating things to do. Rewarding behaviour you like increases the chance of that behaviour happening more often. Here are some ideas you can use to increase your teenager's appropriate behaviour. As you work through Exercises 5 to 7, ask yourself what changes, if any, you feel you need to make to encourage your teenager's desirable behaviour.

praise your teenager

Everyone likes to receive praise, even though some teenagers (and adults) may pretend they do not. Notice what your teenager does, and praise the behaviour you like. With teenagers, it needs to be more subtle than with younger children. Just a few words may be enough, such as *Thanks for keeping the music down while I was on the phone* or *You did a great job of cleaning the car*. But make sure you describe exactly what it was you liked, as this is more effective than just a general *Thanks* or *Well done*. Praise works best when you are enthusiastic and mean what you say. You may get some odd looks at first if this is new to your teenager — but be prepared to persist.

■ exercise 5 how to give descriptive praise

Look at your list of goals for things you would like your teenager to do more often (see page 17). In the space below, write down two of these behaviours that occur occasionally and the descriptive praise you could use to encourage these behaviours. Try to be as specific and descriptive as you can.

Behaviour:

....

....

Descriptive praise:

....

....

Behaviour:

....

....

Descriptive praise:

....

....

give your teenager attention

There are many ways of giving attention. A smile, wink, pat on the back or just watching are all forms of attention that teenagers enjoy and can be used to encourage behaviour you like. These actions add to your praise and show your teenager how pleased you are with their behaviour. You can also use these forms of attention when your teenager is behaving well in situations where you are unable to praise them, such as when they are in a group of friends and your praise may embarrass them. Remember, you can give attention specifically to increase a desirable behaviour, and generally to promote a positive relationship.

■ exercise 6 ways to give attention

Write down some ways you can give attention to your teenager.

....

....

....

....

provide opportunities for engaging activities

Not every parent can afford to buy the latest in computer games, sporting or other equipment. However, it is still important to provide teenagers with opportunities to explore a range of interesting things to do. The local library, community newspaper, and recreation centres often provide information about many opportunities to experience new activities at low cost. You may need to go along for the first few times to help your teenager feel comfortable, or you may decide to do something together, or as a family.

■ exercise 7 ideas for engaging activities

Think of some fun new activities for your teenager. You may like to get some ideas from other people. List some activities for indoors and outdoors.

INDOOR ACTIVITIES	OUTDOOR ACTIVITIES

teaching new skills and behaviours

Finally, parents need to know how to encourage the development of new skills and behaviours. The next section looks at the role of parents as teachers. Growing up involves learning many new independent living and problem-solving skills, such as cooking, getting along with others, and establishing and maintaining relationships. Parents need to know how to help their teenagers learn these skills. Some suggestions are given below. As you work through Exercises 8 to 11, think about what changes, if any, you think you need to make in helping your teenager learn new skills and behaviours.

set a good example

We all learn through watching others. To encourage a new behaviour, plan a time to let your teenager watch you. Describe what you are doing and let your teenager copy your actions. Provide help if necessary and encourage your teenager to try again without any help. Praise your teenager when they are successful.

Do not expect your teenager to behave appropriately if no one else in the family does. For example, you cannot expect your teenager to tidy away after themselves if you leave your own things lying around. Set a good example to show your teenager how to behave.

■ exercise 8 ways to set a good example

From your list of goals for your teenager's behaviour (see page 17), decide if there are any behaviours you can encourage by setting a good example. List them below.

....

....

....

....

coach problem-solving

This is something that can be used when your teenager asks for information, or when they are struggling with a problem. At these times they are often motivated to learn. With younger children, parents usually know or can work out an answer, but with teenagers it may be something neither of you knows the answer to. Even if you do have an answer, try not to give it right away, as this does not help your teenager learn to think for themselves.

With a clear-cut problem, prompt your teenager to come up with the answer, or a way of finding out how to get the answer – *What do you think?* or *How do you think we could find out?* This should be something you can do together. Ensure your teenager does whatever they can to find the answer, but help where you can, and give the answer if they cannot come up with it. There will be lots of opportunities for this type of learning exchange, especially if you are helpful.

There are different types of teaching opportunities that occur frequently. Think of how you could coach your teenager to problem solve in the following situations. What could you say:

When your teenager asks you questions, particularly the common *How?* or *Why?* questions (e.g. *How can I find out what time the next bus goes to town?*).

....

....

When your teenager cannot think of the right word for something (e.g. *What's another way of saying someone is rude?*).

....

....

When your teenager is frustrated with an activity and asks for help (e.g. *I can't work out how to do this!*).

....

....

You may like to refer to page 164 for some suggestions.

If the problem is more complex and there is no clear solution, more time will be needed and you may find it helpful to go through the steps below and show your teenager how to approach a more difficult problem.

goal

Help your teenager to clarify the problem, and agree on what the goal is. What will the situation be like when the problem has been solved?

options

There are usually several of ways a goal can be reached and the first one thought of is not always the best. Consider a range of options before deciding which one has the best chance of achieving the goal.

Together, think of as many possible solutions as you can.

consequences

Before deciding which option to try, first check to see what the likely consequences will be for each option. Sometimes an option will achieve the goal, but have undesirable side-effects that can be noted in advance with a bit of thought. Decide on the best option. Sometimes combining two options brings the best results.

trial it

When the best option has been selected, discuss how to give it every chance of working and then give it a try. It is sometimes best to have a second option ready (Plan B) in case the first does not work as planned.

review

Whether it works or not, it is always a good idea to review what happened. This can be an opportunity to congratulate each other on a good plan, or to try again. Either way it is important to praise cooperation and success. Also, a review can be a good learning experience for the next time a problem comes up.

Think of a recent or current problem that requires more than a single prompt to find a solution. Write down what you might say to your teenager to help them work through the problem-solving steps. You will not be able to complete the final review step unless you actually try out your selected solution.

Problem: ....

GOAL	
OPTIONS	
CONSEQUENCES	
PLAN FOR TRIAL	
REVIEW	

Remember that your job as a parent is not to solve the problem yourself, but to raise important questions, and to make suggestions only when necessary. Your teenager will not learn much about solving problems if you do all the work every time!

use a behaviour contract

When a new behaviour is being learned, you may find it necessary to provide extra motivation until it is firmly established. With teenagers, this can take some weeks and persistence on your part! A behaviour contract can be very useful here. It is an effective short-to-medium term strategy that can be used for a while and then phased out. Your teenager can earn privileges in return for improvements in the desired behaviour. This gives them a sense of achievement and recognition for their efforts. It is most important that the contract be negotiated with your teenager, even though they may not end up fully agreeing with it.

Some parents object to the idea of providing rewards for behaviour that they believe teenagers should just do. The problem is that if the behaviours parents want are not occurring, despite their best efforts at persuasion, the only other options are to use aggressive stand-over tactics, or nag and yell at the teenager until they do what the parent wants. In the longer term, these tactics cause resentment and anger all round, and often lead to serious conflict. Alternatively, parents can just give in and do it themselves. However, the teenager then avoids learning the skills they will need when they leave home to live as an independent adult.

■ exercise 10 using a behaviour contract

Select one or two behaviours you would like to see your teenager do, or do more of, that you do not think other strategies will work for. For many parents this may be a family chore. You may find it helpful to go through the Family Jobs List on the next page and review who currently does the chores in your family, and whether your teenager currently benefits from the efforts of others while doing very little themselves.

Write down tasks from the Family Jobs List (or others) you want your teenager to take more responsibility for doing.

family jobs list

On the left, next to each activity or chore, write the names of the family member/s who currently do or help with each task. On the right of each activity or chore, write the names of any other family member who benefits from it being done. For example, a parent might make everyone's breakfast, so their name goes on the left, and everyone else's name goes on the right. Complete this for all the activities on the list that apply to your family.

WHO CURRENTLY DOES THE CHORE?	ACTIVITY/ CHORE	WHO BENEFITS?
....	Making breakfast	....
....	Making lunch	....
....	Making evening meal	....
....	Shopping for food	....
....	Fixing things that are broken	....
....	Washing the dishes	....
....	Washing clothes	....
....	Ironing clothes	....
....	Mending clothes	....
....	Sweeping/Vacumming	....
....	Putting out garbage	....
....	Cleaning house	....
....	Feeding pets	....
....	Looking after/exercising pets	....
....	Mowing the lawn	....
....	Weeding the garden	....
....	Cleaning the bath/shower	....
....	Cleaning the windows	....
....	Cleaning/washing the car	....
	Any other chores (specify)	
....	....	....
....	....	....
....	....	....

Next, think of what your teenager can receive for improving or increasing the desired behaviour/s. You should discuss this with your teenager to get their ideas on things they would like to work for. Here are some suggestions:

Family activities

- board games (chess, monopoly™)
- card games (500, rummy)
- puzzles (jigsaws, charades)
- social events (bbq, picnic at beach, party)
- eating out (burgers, pizza, seafood)

Other activities

- watching TV
- renting a movie
- computer games
- reading, being read to
- making things (models, something for their room)
- travel, holidays
- swimming, surfing, sailing, skating
- having a haircut/postponing haircut
- going to library, art gallery, museum

Being with

- friends (at their home or yours)
- parents (activity specified by teenager)
- relatives
- animals
- other

Special edibles

- ice cream, chocolate, cool drinks
- favourite meals, desserts, cakes
- special snacks, pizza

Special events

- trips (zoo, wildlife park)
- movies, shows
- sporting event (football, basketball)
- having friends stay over
- sleeping over at a friend's
- shopping, camping out

Buying

- magazines, music
- computer games
- clothes, books
- a pet

Use of

- computer
- TV/DVD player
- telephone
- bike, skateboard, roller blades
- tools, sport equipment
- parent's clothes, jewellery

Remember to choose rewards that you believe your teenager will enjoy.

....

....

....

....

behaviour contract guidelines

Here are some guidelines for constructing a workable behaviour contract to encourage appropriate behaviour:

- Clearly describe the behaviour/s that will be the focus of the contract. State the behaviour positively and include a time statement, such as *Wash the dishes after every evening meal* or *Feed the dog every morning before going to school.*

- Agree on what the rewards will be for improvements in the selected behaviour/s. It is best to match or link the reward to the behaviour. Chores completed around the home might earn the right to watch a favourite TV show, or buy a new magazine. Improvements in helpfulness or politeness might earn the right to choose a preferred take-away meal for Friday night, or select a movie for the family to watch. Compliance with homework requirements or music practice might earn the right to go to a friend's party on the weekend. Some of the best rewards involve activities, such as special time with you, or a family visit to a special place.

- Agree on what level of behaviour will earn what level of reward. Do not expect new behaviours to be learned perfectly at first. Reward improvement over past levels, rather than aiming for instant perfection. If your teenager makes an extra effort, but then does not earn a reward, the motivation to keep trying will fade and no lasting change will occur. You can always make changes to the contract in later weeks that require your teenager to improve more to earn the reward.

- If the behaviour is one that just has to occur, such as being ready on time to go to school, a back-up penalty for not succeeding may be necessary. It is generally much better to rely on rewards to improve desirable behaviour, but sometimes it will be necessary to arrange a penalty for missing deadlines.

- Select rewards that are practical and within your budget. If your teenager wants a large reward (such as a new bike), spread it over several weeks or months. For example, get a picture of a bike and cut it up into, say, 20 pieces – then stick the picture together piece by piece as each piece is earned. This also allows you time to save up. However, small rewards given daily are much better than large rewards given weeks or months later. Sometimes it is appropriate to arrange both. The small rewards keep the new behaviour going on a daily basis, and the large reward keeps it going over a period of weeks. Also it is a good idea to have a range of rewards to choose from to prevent your teenager getting bored with just one. A reward can lose its effect over time if it is obtained too often or is too far off.

- Select rewards that you have control over. It is pointless to agree to extra TV or computer time, if your teenager has their own TV or computer in their room to use whenever they like. Similarly, it is no use offering to pay them a small amount every time they mow the lawn if they have a part time job and earn a much larger regular amount.

- Make sure that whatever reward you promise, you can deliver it. Nothing undermines a behaviour contract more than not getting the agreed reward. Imagine how you would feel if an employer did not pay as promised, or a friend cheated on a loan! If there is a possibility that this could happen, make sure you discuss it immediately and arrange a way of making it up.

- Finally, make it clear that the agreed behaviour must occur before the agreed reward can be enjoyed. Do not give in to threats or promises or the contract will not work.

The next step is to specify what behaviour will earn what reward. There are lots of different ways to organise this. Some are quite simple, and others are more complicated. Try and keep it simple to start with. There are two examples provided in the example contracts #1A and #1B on the next pages.

Link the behaviour you want to see more of with the reward you have agreed with your teenager. Remember to set moderately easy goals at first so your teenager is rewarded for their extra effort, then you can gradually make the goals harder to achieve.

....

....

....

....

....

Finally, list anything you need to purchase or organise before you can start using the contract.

....

....

....

....

....

Before putting a behaviour contract into effect there are two final steps. Agree on the contract details, and prepare a monitoring chart to track progress through the week. Write down the agreement and get everyone to sign. It may seem unnecessary, but it prevents an argument later, when it may be hard to remember what was agreed.

There are two example contracts and monitoring charts on the next two pages to give you an idea what they look like.

If the new behaviour improves and the target is reached, you must provide the agreed reward for the system to work. If another problem occurs do not punish your teenager by withholding the earned reward. Negotiate a separate new contract to deal with the new problem. You may get some ideas from the next section on Managing Problem Behaviour, which also recommends the use of behaviour contracts, but with some additional features.

example behaviour contract #1a

Between: John and Mum

Starting on: Monday 12th June

Behaviour/chore: John will make his bed and clean up his room before 7.30a.m. on schooldays and before breakfast on non-school days.

Reward: Watch one hour of TV after school between 5p.m. and 6p.m. (or anytime on weekends and holidays).

Conditions: If jobs not completed on time, no TV permitted that day before 6p.m.

example monitoring chart #1a

Name: John   Week beginning: Monday 12th June

ACTIVITY & DETAILS	CARRY OVER	M	T	W	T	F	S	S	TOTAL
Make bed, and clean up room, before breakfast daily	N/A	✗	✓	✓	✓	✗	✗	✓	4

In this example John did not complete his chore on Monday morning so he did not get to watch TV that afternoon. Tuesday he did better and he got to watch TV that afternoon. Wednesday and Thursday he did okay too, but Friday and Saturday he missed out again. Sunday he did okay again so he ended up with 4 days out of 7. That is not bad for the first week, but we might want to improve on that next week.

The monitoring chart allows you to check off when rewards are earned, and to keep track of progress. This is an important part of the behaviour contract as it enables you to monitor whether the contract is working. Changes may need to be made if the new behaviour is not occurring, or the jobs are not being done at agreed times, or to an acceptable standard. The monitoring chart needs to be pinned up in a place where it can be easily seen and where it can be easily written on. It is best to have a rule that only parents are allowed to write on the monitoring chart.

In the second example a points system is used to check on a number of separate behaviours. This is a little more complicated, but is more flexible. Jane is to clean away the dirty dishes after the evening meal, stack the dishwasher, and feed the dog each day. After talking to Jane, it is agreed that she can exchange the points she earns for time on the telephone with friends to a maximum of 60 minutes on any school day. Each point earns her 10 minutes of telephone time. The contract is shown on the next page, and the monitoring chart shows how the week went.

example behaviour contract #1b

Between: Jane and Dad

Starting on: Monday 12th June

Behaviour/chore: Jane will clear away dishes after the evening meal, stack the dishwasher before 8pm, and feed the dog each day before breakfast.

Reward: Clearing away dishes = 3pts; Stacking dishwasher = 2 points; Feeding the dog = 1 point. Each point may be exchanged for 10 mins of telephone time.

Conditions: No credit allowed, but unused points may be carried over to the next day. Telephone calls may be made to a maximum of 60 minutes between 6p.m. and 9p.m. on schooldays. No more than 1 hour of telephone time can be carried over to the following week.

example monitoring chart #1b

Name: Jane   **Week beginning:** Monday 12th June

ACTIVITY & DETAILS	CARRY OVER	M	T	W	T	F	S	S	TOTAL
Clear away dishes (3pts)		0	3	0	0	3	0	0	2
Stack dishwasher (2pts)		2	0	0	2	0	0	2	3
Feed dog (1pt)		1	1	1	1	1	0	1	6
TOTAL EARNED PER DAY		3	4	1	3	4	0	3	
1pt = 10 mins phone time:									
Time earned		30	40	10	30	40	0	30	3hrs
Time used		60	40	0	40	40	0	30	3hrs
Time remaining	30	0	0	10	0	0	0	0	0

On Monday, Jane stacked the dishwasher and earned 2 points and fed the dog for another 1 point. She earned 3 points for the day which she could exchange for 30 minutes of telephone time. However, as she had carried over 30 minutes from the previous week she had 60 minutes available. She used up all that time to talk to her friends for 1 hour that evening so she had no phone time left.

On Tuesday, she cleared away the dishes and again fed the dog. Her 4 points earned her 40 minutes of telephone time, which she used up that evening. On Wednesday, she only fed the dog to earn 10 minutes of phone time, which she didn't use. On Thursday, she stacked the dishwasher and fed the dog and earned another 30 minutes. She added the 10 minutes she had earned the day before and used it all up on Thursday evening. On Friday she earned another 40 minutes of phone time and used it all. On Saturday she did none of her chores and had no phone time that day. Finally, on Sunday she earned another 30 minutes of phone time and used it all that evening.

Over the week shown in the example, Jane cleared the dishes away twice, stacked the dishwasher three times, and fed the dog on six of the days. In return she was able to talk to her friends on the phone for a total of 3 hours. Telephone time certainly seems important to Jane as she uses it regularly. However, the jobs that have to do with the dishes are not being done regularly. The point value of these jobs may need to be increased, or perhaps the amount of time on the telephone that each point earns may need to be reduced. This may look complicated, but it is much more flexible as it allows you to give points for several different behaviours that you want a teenager to do, and use a single monitoring chart to record the points they earn that can be exchanged for rewards. You may wish to provide a choice of rewards with different point values too.

family meetings

Working out family problems and writing behaviour contracts can take a bit of time and cannot be done in a hurry. Many families often discover there are few occasions when they come together to discuss matters of importance, or simply to enjoy talking to each other. One way to address this is to organise a family meeting for an appropriate time during the week. This will give the message that you are serious about dealing with these matters, and increases the chances that they will be well done and will work. Family meetings do not need to be long and boring, although this may be the initial reaction to the idea, especially by teenagers. It is therefore important to make them brief, focused, and as enjoyable as possible. Here are some suggestions about planning and holding family meetings:

- If possible, pick a time when everyone can be present on a regular weekly basis, and keep to it. Select a time when people are not too tired, and not right after or before other commitments to avoid rushing. Sometimes you may need to change the time, or accept that someone cannot make it, but aim for a regular meeting time.
- Pick a setting that is comfortable and away from other distractions (TV, radio). Each family member should be able to see everyone else. Around the dining table is a good place for many families.
- Take the meeting seriously and have a set agenda so that everyone knows what is going to be discussed, but allow people to bring other issues up as well. (See the example agenda on page 52.)
- Set time limits for meetings. Perhaps start with 15 minutes to get people used to the idea, and then increase the time gradually as needed. It is rarely a good idea to meet for as long as an hour unless there is a big problem to work on.
- Discourage visitors and telephone calls during meeting times. Either switch the answering machine on, unplug the telephone, or tell people who phone that you will call back later. Remove or turn off other possible distractions such as TV and radio, although some peaceful background music may be suitable if everyone agrees.
- Agree on rules for the meeting. If someone needs to leave the meeting, ask permission; *Only one person at a time can speak*; *Speak quietly*, are some examples that you might wish to use.
- Stop the meeting if any one person makes more than three hostile comments or rule violations. Deal with the problem away from the meeting, and hold the meeting later, with or without the offending person.
- Always invite everyone but do not force anyone to attend. If problem behaviour continues, think about setting up a behaviour contract.
- It can be helpful to nominate different people for different jobs. A chairperson can make sure people keep to the agenda. A recorder can write down any decisions that are made. A time-keeper can make sure there is enough time to discuss every item, and a mediator can help people to keep to the rules. It is

best to rotate these jobs so that everyone gets a chance in each job. That way everyone learns more and feels involved.

- If possible, arrange for a pleasant family activity to follow the family meeting, such as a family game, snack, or movie.
- Family meetings can also be used to discuss the coming week, organise weekends and holidays, or deal with issues that keep getting put off. As family members experience benefits from sitting down to plan together, they may be more willing to participate.

■ exercise 11 planning a family meeting

Think about when you could hold a family meeting. You may like to call a family meeting to discuss the behaviour contract you are planning. Write down a few suitable times to discuss with other members of your family.

....

....

....

....

....

....

....

summary

During Week 2, 10 positive parenting strategies were introduced. These included:

- spending time with your teenager
- talking to your teenager
- showing affection
- praising your teenager
- giving your teenager attention
- providing opportunities for engaging activities
- setting a good example
- coaching problem-solving
- using a behaviour contract
- holding a family meeting

Think about which of these strategies you would like to use with your teenager.

practice tasks

- Choose two strategies to try out with your teenager. Set specific goals such as *I will use descriptive praise three times each day* and *I will find a time at least once a day for us to talk together.*

Write down the two strategies you plan to use over the next 7 days.

....

....

....

....

- Keep track of how you go by using the checklist on page 51. Each day, write 'Y' for Yes or 'N' for No in the column under each goal. A space is provided for writing any comments, reactions or obstacles to reaching your daily goals (e.g. *Jamie seemed to like being praised* or *Late home and too tired today*). An additional copy of this form is provided in the Worksheets section.

- Hold a family meeting (see the example agenda on page 52) to discuss the Family Jobs List (page 53) and redraft the behaviour contract you have begun to write (use the blank form on page 54). Implement the contract after you and your teenager have both signed it and set up a monitoring chart.

- Continue monitoring the behaviours you selected earlier (page 25) and keep track of progress on the recording form and the behaviour graph.

For a review of the material covered this week, you may like to watch:

- *Every Parent's Guide to Teenagers*, Part 3, Encouraging Appropriate Behaviour.

content of next week

During Week 3 you will look at practical strategies for managing problem behaviour and helping teenagers to develop self-control.

checklist for encouraging appropriate behaviour

Choose two of the strategies introduced in Week 2 that you would like to practise with your teenager over the next week. Be as specific as possible (e.g. one goal may be to use descriptive praise statements with your teenager at least three times per day). Use the table below to record whether you reached your goals each day. Comment on what went well and list any problems that occurred.

GOAL 1:

....

....

GOAL 2:

....

....

DAY	GOAL 1 Y/N	GOAL 2 Y/N	COMMENTS
1			
2			
3			
4			
5			
6			
7			

example agenda for family meeting #1

Preparation

- agree on time and place for meeting; agree on realistic time-limit (e.g. 30 minutes)
- gather all relevant material together from noticeboard, etc.
- appoint chairperson, timekeeper and recorder

Agenda

- *item 1:* discuss Family Jobs List and new behaviours/chores for teenager
- *item 2:* discuss possible rewards that will be linked to new behaviours/chores
- *item 3:* negotiate draft Behaviour Contract #1 (do not implement)
- *item 4:* draw up Monitoring Chart
- *item 5:* any other business
- *item 6:* set time for next meeting

Before closing the meeting, quickly review any important decisions that have been made.

Afterwards

Where possible, organise some brief pleasant activity for all family members to do together to reward everyone for taking part in the family meeting.

family jobs list

On the left, next to each activity or chore, write the names of the family member/s who currently do or help with each task. On the right of each activity or chore, write the names of any other family member who benefits from it being done. For example, a parent might make everyone's breakfast, so their name goes on the left, and everyone else's name goes on the right. Complete this for all the activities on the list that apply to your family.

WHO CURRENTLY DOES THE CHORE?	ACTIVITY/ CHORE	WHO BENEFITS?
....	Making breakfast	....
....	Making lunch	....
....	Making evening meal	....
....	Shopping for food	....
....	Fixing things that are broken	....
....	Washing the dishes	....
....	Washing clothes	....
....	Ironing clothes	....
....	Mending clothes	....
....	Sweeping/Vacumming	....
....	Putting out garbage	....
....	Cleaning house	....
....	Feeding pets	....
....	Looking after/exercising pets	....
....	Mowing the lawn	....
....	Weeding the garden	....
....	Cleaning the bath/shower	....
....	Cleaning the windows	....
....	Cleaning/washing the car	....
....	Any other chores (specify)	....
....	....	....
....	....	....
....	....	....

behaviour contract #1

Between: .... and: ....

Starting on: .... (date) ....

Behaviour/chore: ....

....

....

....

Reward: ....

....

....

Conditions: ....

....

....

monitoring chart #1

Name: .... Week beginning: ....

ACTIVITY & DETAILS	CARRY OVER	M	T	W	T	F	S	S	TOTAL

managing problem behaviour

overview

All teenagers need to learn to accept limits and to control their disappointment when they do not get what they want. Managing these situations can be challenging for parents, particularly if this has been a problem during a teenager's younger years. However, there are positive and effective ways to help teenagers learn self-control, and defer short-term benefits in favour of longer-term goals. Teenagers learn self-control when their parents use consequences for problem behaviour immediately, consistently and decisively. This week, several options for managing teenagers' problem behaviour that parents may have to deal with at home will be presented. Consider each as an option you could use with your family. During Week 7, strategies for dealing with more risky behaviour that may occur outside the home will be introduced.

By the end of Week 3 you should be able to:

- Set appropriate family rules and discuss them with your family.
- Use directed discussion to deal with mild problem behaviour.
- Make clear, calm requests.
- Back up your requests with logical consequences.
- Deal calmly with emotional behaviour.
- Put into practice a behaviour contract to manage problem behaviour.

review of progress

■ exercise 1 review use of strategies

What were your practice tasks from last week (refer to page 50)?

....

....

....

What worked? Please be specific and think of at least two positive points. It may be helpful to look at your checklist for encouraging appropriate behaviour (page 51).

....

....

....

Is there anything that you could have done differently? You may notice some steps on your checklist that you missed or could improve.

....

....

....

What might you need to practise further?

....

....

....

managing problem behaviour

Last week, strategies were introduced to encourage appropriate behaviour. Although this may also lead to a reduction in problem behaviour, some problem behaviour may not respond to these strategies alone. Effective discipline strategies may also be needed and a number of strategies for helping teenagers deal with frustration and accept limits are presented in this section. Each strategy is presented as an option for you to consider. You may have heard about and already use some of them, and some may be new to you. All strategies have their limitations and no single strategy will work for all situations. Sometimes several strategies are needed in combination. It is important to recognise that the strategies introduced here for managing problem behaviour will be ineffective if your teenager does not receive positive attention and encouragement for behaving appropriately. These strategies therefore need to be used in conjunction with the strategies covered in Week 2 if they are to be effective. Use this as a chance to think about your approach to discipline and to fine-tune it. The principles of effective discipline are immediacy, consistency, and decisiveness. Ask yourself these questions:

- *Do I have a discipline strategy that works?*
- *Do I have a back up if my first line of approach doesn't work?*
- *How effective is it? Is the problem behaviour occurring less often?*
- *Does it teach my teenager how they are expected to behave?*

As you look at each strategy and work through the exercises, think about when the strategy could be used in your family.

establishing clear family rules

Teenagers need limits so they know what is expected of them and how they should behave. A few basic family rules (no more than four or five) can help. Rules should tell teenagers what to do, rather than what not to do. *Walk in the house, Speak in a pleasant voice* and *Keep your hands and feet to yourself* are better rules than *Don't run, Don't shout* and *Don't fight*. Rules work best when they are fair, easy to follow, and you can back them up. Try to involve your teenager in deciding on family rules. The key points to remember are:

- have a small number of rules
- rules should be fair
- rules should be easy to follow
- rules should be enforceable
- rules should be positively stated

Below are some rules that other parents have selected. They are all stated positively with the problem behaviour included in brackets as a guide.

example family rules

- be honest (not untruthful)
- be polite (not rude)
- be assertive (not aggressive or too passive)
- be reliable (not unreliable)
- be gentle (not rough)
- be kind (not mean or hurtful)

- be positive and constructive (not negative or destructive)
- be helpful and considerate (not unhelpful or inconsiderate)
- speak quietly (not yelling or shouting)
- respect others' property and privacy (not taking things or going into rooms without asking)

▨ exercise 2 establishing clear rules

In the space provided, list up to four or five rules that you would like to use in your home.

....

....

....

....

....

use directed discussion to deal with rule breaking

Even when you have a set of family rules that everyone knows, your teenager may 'forget' and break the rule. Sometimes, especially when a new rule has just been agreed, you can use directed discussion to remind the teenager what they are meant to do. It involves gaining their attention, specifying the behaviour of concern, asking for the rule to be stated, and then requiring the correct behaviour.

For example – *Joan, you are speaking too loudly. What's our rule about how to speak to each other?... OK, now let's start again and follow that rule.* And when they follow the rule, make sure you praise them – *Thank you for following the rule.*

▨ exercise 3 using directed discussion to deal with rule breaking

Think of a rule that occasionally gets broken in your house or imagine that your teenager has just broken one of your new rules. Write down what you could say to your teenager at each step of a directed discussion to teach your teenager the correct behaviour.

Situation:

....

....

Gain your teenager's attention:

....

....

State the problem briefly, simply and calmly:

....

....

Briefly restate why the behaviour is a problem:

....

....

Ask your teenager to tell you the rule and state the correct behaviour:

....

....

....

....

Request that your teenager follow the rule and practise the correct behaviour:

....

....

Praise your teenager for the correct behaviour:

....

....

If your teenager continually fails to follow the rule, you may need to consider setting up a behaviour contract (see pages 70–73).

make clear, calm requests

As well as expecting teenagers to follow family rules, there will be occasions when parents want their teenager to cooperate with their requests. The way requests are made influences whether a teenager will cooperate or not – and whether or not parents have to deal with problem behaviour.

When making a request of a teenager it is important to be polite, clear, and specific. However, it is not reasonable to always insist on instant obedience. As children get older, give them more freedom to complete a required task when it suits them, within reason, although you should still set time limits. However, if a problem behaviour is occurring that you want to stop, act immediately. When you want your teenager to do something right away, be prepared to back up your request if it is not carried out.

When you want your teenager to cooperate, follow these steps:

get your timing right

No one likes being interrupted when they are involved in something important or enjoyable. Give advance notice where possible – *Please be ready to go out in 20 minutes.*

get close and gain your teenager's attention

Stop what you are doing and move so they can easily see and hear you. Use their name to gain their attention.

describe what you want your teenager to do

Be specific, and say exactly what you want them to do — *Peter, please turn off the TV at seven o'clock because I'm putting dinner on the table then.*

give your teenager time to cooperate

Allow enough time for your teenager to do what you asked.

praise cooperation

If your teenager cooperates with your request, praise them — *Thank you for turning the TV off and coming to the table as I asked Peter.*

provide a back-up consequence for non-cooperation

If your teenager does not cooperate, do not give a second chance. This may be appropriate with younger children, but older children should have learned to do what is asked at the first time of asking. This is expected at school, at work, and in other adult relationships. Back-up your request with a consequence. Never threaten to apply a consequence as this will teach your teenager only to respond to your requests when a threat is included. Threats also increase the emotional temperature and make an argument more likely. Suggestions about what consequences might be used, and how to apply them, are covered in Exercise 5 (page 62).

■ exercise 4 making clear, calm requests

Your teenager's TV time allocation is used up but they continue to watch it.

....

....

Your teenager is interrupting your telephone call by turning the TV up quite loud.

....

....

Your teenager's wet towels and swimsuit are scattered on the floor.

....

....

Your teenager is yelling at a younger sibling to return something they borrowed.

....

....

Your teenager is eating a snack in front of the TV, and food scraps are being spilled on to the carpet.

....

....

You may like to refer to page 165 to check your ideas.

back up your requests with logical consequences

Grounding teenagers for lengthy periods when they misbehave does not work well. First, it usually punishes you as well because you have to monitor your teenager closely to make the grounding work. Second, many parents give in before the time is over – your teenager then learns that you do not mean what you say. Third, taking away your teenager's freedom is a very powerful penalty. Once you do this, you cannot use it again until you give it back. And finally, it is important to give your teenager an opportunity to demonstrate they have learned to behave better. Therefore, impose a brief, but appropriate consequence, and then allow your teenager the opportunity to show they have learned. If they have not, you can always impose the consequence again.

Logical consequences are best used for behaviour problems that do not occur too often. If your teenager does not follow a clear request, choose a consequence that fits the situation if you can. If possible, remove the activity or equipment that is at the centre of the problem. Logical consequences work best if they are brief – 15 to 30 minutes is usually long enough the first time. When a problem occurs, follow these steps:

withdraw the activity

Do not debate or argue the point. Act as soon as the problem occurs. Explain why you are removing access to the activity – *You are not sharing this computer game with your younger brother as agreed so I'm switching it off for 15 minutes* or *You haven't turned the sound down on the radio as I asked, so I'm switching it off for 30 minutes.*

return the activity

Remember to keep to the agreement. When the time is up, return the activity so your teenager can practise how to behave appropriately. Try to prevent the same thing happening again by coaching them on how to solve the problem.

use another consequence if necessary

If a problem occurs again within the next hour or so after returning the activity, follow up by removing the activity for a longer period, such as the rest of the day.

If the problem occurs regularly, consider setting up a behaviour contract to deal with it. The section on using behaviour contracts to manage problem behaviour is covered later in this session – see page 70.

■ exercise 5 backing up your requests with logical consequences

Think of some logical consequences for the following situations and make a note of what you would say to your teenager:

Your teenager is playing music too loudly and hasn't followed your request to turn it down.

....

....

Your teenager has borrowed their brother's computer game without permission and ignores your request that they should go and ask him.

....

....

Your teenager is arguing loudly with a sibling about which TV channel to watch and ignores your suggestion that they solve the problem in a friendly and quiet way.

....

....

Your teenager borrowed your bike, and despite your request that they put it away, has left it out in the rain.

....

....

You may like to refer to page 165 to check your ideas.

If your teenager argues with you about the consequence, or turns the music/TV/ computer back on before the time limit is up, you will need to apply a back-up consequence (*e.g. You haven't accepted the consequence so now I'm going to put the TV/ CD player away until tomorrow or so now you won't be allowed out this evening*). You will need to think ahead to make sure you are not penalising other members of the family unfairly, and that you can actually do what you say you will do. This may require some planning and support from your partner (if you have one) or from others. If your teenager becomes very angry and emotional, you will need to use the routine for dealing with a teenager's emotions described in the next section on pages 63 to 69.

acknowledging teenagers' emotions

Dealing with teenagers' emotions can be very difficult for parents. Teenagers can become emotional quite quickly when things happen they cannot control. This typically includes being angry, fearful, or sad. These occasions are important as they provide opportunities for you to help your teenager learn to cope with the disappointments and frustrations that they will face throughout life. If you have already been doing this during their early years, it will be so much easier as the problems they face get bigger. If this is new to you, it will be more difficult, but that makes it more important than ever that you learn now, while you can still help.

When a teenager seems upset by something, stay calm, acknowledge how they are feeling and see if you can find out why they are upset; do not try to work out what you might do to help while they are upset.

The first thing to do when you become aware that your teenager is distressed is to stop what you are doing and pay attention to your teenager. While your teenager is talking, stay silent, but listen closely to what they are saying. Do not interrupt, tell them they are wrong, or try to make them feel better. You may ask a clarifying question if you are having trouble following what they are saying. However, it is more important to show you are listening than trying to understand all the details at this point.

When you think they have finished, briefly summarise what you think your teenager has told you, but use your own words. Check with them to see whether you got it right. Try to help your teenager put a name to the feeling – once they have learned to label a feeling accurately, it is easier to talk about and deal with. Reassure your teenager it is okay to feel that way – perhaps share a time when you last felt that way too, but do not use that to distract your teenager from their own experience. Be cautious when labelling your teenager's emotions. It is often better to make tentative suggestions – *Sounds like you're mad at your brother?* This allows the teenager to give a different label if it does not quite fit – *No, it's just that I'm disappointed he let me down.* It is often difficult trying to put labels on other people's feelings, but if handled with care, it can be very helpful.

The most important thing is to validate their emotion – tell your teenager that it is quite natural for them to have these feelings. At this stage, simply summarise and reflect what you hear – do not try to solve the problem, or pass it off as trivial or unimportant.

After reaching this point, and only if your teenager has begun to calm down, you might want to help them to problem solve. Do not make that decision yourself, but ask them what they want you to do. The challenge now is to give your teenager just as much help as they need, but not to take over. Your teenager needs to learn how to manage their emotions for themselves. Your job is to support and encourage them as they struggle with this task, but not to do it for them.

They may want you to just listen, to help them cope with their current feelings, or perhaps to help set a goal for change. If you think they want to problem solve, prompt them through the steps: clarify the goal, select a potential solution, and come up with a plan to try out (refer back to pages 38 to 40 for more detail).

If your teenager does not respond to your suggestions, or directs their frustration at you, suggest a cooling off period, and set a time to talk again. If they reject your offer of help, or say they can manage themselves, respect that but make it clear you are available to help later on if they change their mind. If you believe they are going to need help to solve their problem, offer again later when they are calmer.

■ exercise 6 preparing to deal calmly with teenagers' emotions

Think of a recent example when your teenager was distressed about something.

What could you say to your teenager when you notice they are distressed about something?

....

....

What could you say to your teenager to show you are listening?

....

....

What could you say to your teenager to show you understand they are feeling emotional?

....

....

When should you ask your teenager if you can help?

....

....

What could you say to your teenager if they have calmed down and want you to help them sort things out?

....

....

What could you say to your teenager if they have not calmed down or do not want your help?

....

....

You may wish to refer to page 166 to check your ideas.

developing parenting routines

Sometimes teenagers' emotions are brief and do not require any further action by the parent. At other times these emotional reactions may continue or escalate and need to be dealt with. The flow chart below shows how to put together some strategies to create a routine for dealing with emotional behaviour. This routine is useful when you have to deal with emotional behaviour, particularly if it has resulted from a disagreement with you. This can typically occur when your teenager is trying to avoid doing something you have asked them to do, or when you have refused to let them do something they want to do. By following this routine you can break the escalation trap where parent and teenager become increasingly angry or upset before one or the other gives in or storms off in a temper. It is likely that you will remain calm and your teenager will be less likely to escalate if you follow these steps.

routine for dealing with emotional behaviour

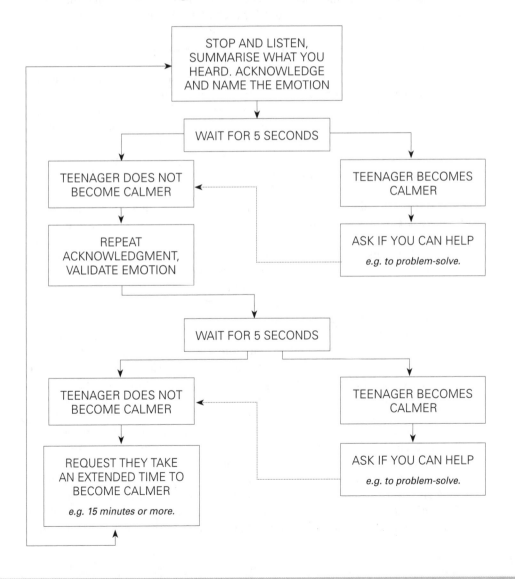

STOP AND LISTEN, SUMMARISE WHAT YOU HEARD. ACKNOWLEDGE AND NAME THE EMOTION

WAIT FOR 5 SECONDS

TEENAGER DOES NOT BECOME CALMER

TEENAGER BECOMES CALMER

REPEAT ACKNOWLEDGMENT, VALIDATE EMOTION

ASK IF YOU CAN HELP
e.g. to problem-solve.

WAIT FOR 5 SECONDS

TEENAGER DOES NOT BECOME CALMER

TEENAGER BECOMES CALMER

REQUEST THEY TAKE AN EXTENDED TIME TO BECOME CALMER
e.g. 15 minutes or more.

ASK IF YOU CAN HELP
e.g. to problem-solve.

points to remember

- When your teenager becomes angry or upset, stop what you are doing if you can, look at them, and just listen to what they are saying.
- Try to pick out the key point or points, and when they pause, summarise what you thought they said — *So what I hear you saying is that you're upset because I won't let you go to the party on the weekend?* Use an enquiring tone, rather than saying it as a statement of fact — this allows your teenager to correct any misunderstanding and shows that you have really been listening.
- Acknowledge, and if possible, name the emotion — *Well I can hear that you're really angry with me and disappointed at missing out on this party.*
- Pause for at least 5 seconds to give your teenager time to calm down. Do not say anything, and especially do not try to solve the problem, or change your mind, or dismiss your teenager's emotions as trivial or unimportant.
- If your teenager calms down, ask what they want you to do — *Is there any way I can help?* Guide them towards problem solving, using the strategy described on pages 38 to 40. Remember that your aim is to help them come up with a solution themselves and not to do it for them. Give them as much help as they need, but no more.
- If the issue is about a decision you have made, your teenager might ask you to change your mind. At this point you have several options.
  (1) You may decide to keep to your original decision, and in this case you might want to discuss how your teenager could take part in an alternative event. For example, if your teenager is disappointed at not going to a party because they will not have a chance to spend time with their friends, perhaps you could suggest a small party at your own home, or some other social event you could help organise. You might find it helpful to review the strategy for providing opportunities for engaging activities that was discussed in Week 2 (page 36).
  (2) You may decide that your teenager could take part in some of the activity they are wanting to attend, but not all of it. For example, you might suggest that you are willing to allow them to go to the party, but insist that they must come home at a certain time and that you will pick them up to ensure this occurs. In order to ensure that you have a clear agreement with your teenager about any arrangement you decide on, you may find it helpful to review the strategy of using a behaviour contract that was discussed in Week 2 (page 41).
  (3) The third option is to reconsider whether your original decision was hasty or unreasonable and to now allow them to go. If you choose this option, you must ensure that you make this decision only after a period of calm discussion with your teenager. If you change your mind while your teenager is being emotional, or soon afterwards, they may learn that the way to get you to change your mind is to turn on their emotional behaviour. You may then find this happening more and more often.
- If your teenager does not calm down after you have waited for 5 seconds, simply repeat your acknowledgment, using slightly different words if you can — *Peter, I can see how upset you are about this, you're really angry aren't you?* Then go on and validate the emotion — *I can understand that you're disappointed — it's a perfectly natural reaction.* This gives your teenager the message that you are not criticising them for the way they feel and helps them

to accept the feeling and separate it from what they might want to do about it.

- It is not possible to talk about a problem calmly and rationally when one person is emotionally aroused. Humans have the ability to respond emotionally when something happens that we do not like, as well as to rationally think through a problem and come up with a solution. However, these are two separate processes and they interfere with each other. If you stay calm and focused on solving a problem, you cannot be angry at the same time. But if you are angry and upset, you cannot focus your thoughts on solving a problem. As the parent, you can help your teenager to learn this by staying calm yourself, and avoiding the escalation trap (see page 6 for a review of the escalation trap).

- After repeating the acknowledgment and validating your teenager's emotions, again pause for at least 5 seconds to give your teenager time to calm down. Do not say anything, and again do not try to solve the problem, change your mind, or dismiss your teenager's emotions as trivial or unimportant.

- If your teenager still does not calm down, suggest that further discussion now will not be useful and a cooling off period is the best option – *You still seem very angry and I don't think we should talk any more until you've calmed down; how about you go to your room for 30 minutes – then we'll try again.*

- Keep to the agreement, and when you meet again, repeat the routine. You would now be hoping to just go down the shorter, right-hand side of the routine and have a calm discussion about what to do.

- If your teenager resists your suggestion to take some time to cool off and tries to insist on discussing the issue while they are still upset, initiate it yourself – *Well, I'm now starting to feel angry and I don't want to talk to you while I'm feeling that way; so I'm going to take the dog for a walk and I'll talk to you again in 30 minutes when I get back.*

- If your teenager starts to become emotional or aggressive at any point in the routine, follow the flow chart which suggests that you simply repeat the acknowledgment and validate the emotion, and pause for at least 5 seconds.

exercise 7 using the routine for dealing with emotional behaviour

Try to practise this routine with another adult before using it with your teenager. This practice exercise can help you decide whether this is a routine you would feel comfortable using with your teenager. It also gives you a chance to practise the words you would actually say to your teenager before having to do so.

To set up a practice exercise you will need to find another person to play the role of your teenager. If there are two parents or adults in your family you might like to do this with them. Walk through the steps of the routine as though you were talking to your teenager. The first time you practise the routine, imagine that your teenager does indeed calm down after you have listened to them and acknowledged the emotion. On the next practice, have the person playing your teenager continue to be angry or upset so that you can practise suggesting a calming down period of time-out.

Sometimes, teenagers may have learned that emotional behaviour helps them to escape or avoid things they do not want to do. In these situations, it is best to ignore them, or perhaps prompt them to try something more constructive. If the emotional response is directed at you, the parent, the most important thing is to try and stay calm. Once you have listened to your teenager, they may be able to move to problem solving. Sometimes a parent will need to make it very clear on several occasions that the emotional behaviour is not going to help solve the problem, that it is up to the teenager to suggest a better solution, and that you are willing to assist them to problem solve when they are ready.

■ exercise 8 preparing to deal with manipulative behaviour

Think of recent examples when your teenager may have been using their apparent distress to avoid something, or to get you to do something for them they really should do themselves. You may wish to refer to the example routines on page 69.

What could you say to your teenager if they complain they cannot do something you know they can?

....

....

What could you say to your teenager if they ask you to do something that they should really do for themselves?

....

....

What could you say to your teenager if they shout at you that you should fix their problem for them?

....

....

You may wish to refer to page 167 to check your ideas.

routines for dealing with teenagers' emotional behaviour

UPSET BY SOMEONE OUTSIDE THE FAMILY	UPSET BY SOMEONE INSIDE THE FAMILY	UPSET AT YOU	MANIPULATING
Stop what you are doing and listen to what your teenager is saying. When they have finished speaking, paraphrase what you heard them say. Check to make sure you've got it right.	Stop what you are doing and listen to what your teenager is saying. When they have finished speaking, paraphrase what you heard them say. Check to make sure you've got it right.	Stop what you are doing and listen to what your teenager is saying. When they have finished speaking, paraphrase what you heard them say. Check to make sure you've got it right.	Listen to what your teenager is saying. When they have finished speaking, ignore the emotional behaviour, and prompt them to consider other ways to deal with the problem.
Acknowledge and name the emotion – *Sounds like you're really upset that she let you down?*	Acknowledge and name the emotion – *Sounds like you're really angry that Ben took your gear?*	Acknowledge and name the emotion – *You're really mad at me aren't you?*	Suggest that the emotional behaviour is inappropriate – *That isn't going to solve the problem is it?*
If they are very upset, give them time to cool down. Then, perhaps share a similar experience of your own – *I remember the last time that happened to me...*	If they are very upset, suggest they take time to cool down – *Let's talk about how to fix this when you've cooled down a bit?*	If they are very upset, suggest they take time to cool down – *How about we talk about this in a while when you're not so angry?*	If they continue to show emotional behaviour, continue to ignore it. Tell them you will help when they show interest in finding a solution – *I'm ready to help when you want me to.*
When they have calmed down, ask your teenager what they would like you to do – *What do you want me to do?*	When they have calmed down, ask your teenager what they would like you to do – *What do you want me to do?*	When they have calmed down, ask your teenager what they would like you to do – *What do you want me to do?*	If your teenager approaches you about finding a solution, ask them what they want to do – *What do you think you might do?*
If your teenager does not want your help, make an open offer – *If you want to talk about it later, let me know.*	If your teenager does not want your help, make an open offer – *If you want to talk about it later, let me know.*	If your teenager does not want to talk, make an open offer – *If you want to talk about it later, let me know.*	If your teenager does not want your help, make an open offer – *If you want to talk about it later, let me know.*
If your teenager accepts your offer of help, then or later, coach them to problem solve – *Well, what do you want to happen now?*	If your teenager accepts your offer of help, then or later, coach them to problem solve – *Well, what do you want to happen now?*	If your teenager accepts your offer to talk, then or later, coach them to problem solve – *Well, what do you want to happen now?*	If your teenager accepts your offer of help, then or later, coach them to problem solve – *Well, what is it you're supposed to do?*
Praise them for dealing appropriately with their emotions.	Praise them for dealing appropriately with their emotions.	Praise them for dealing appropriately with their emotions.	Praise them for dealing appropriately with their emotions.

week 3

use a behaviour contract to manage problem behaviour

If your teenager has difficulty following the new rules or controlling their emotions, and directed discussion or these other strategies do not work, you may need to set up a behaviour contract. This will help the new behaviours to become established.

It is often difficult to keep track of rule-following. Rule-breaking is much easier to notice. One way to deal with this problem is to award points in advance on a daily basis, say 3 points per rule per day. If you have 4 rules, this means that your teenager could earn 84 points per week ($3 \times 4 \times 7$). Each instance of rule breaking loses 1 point, and these are deducted from the daily or weekly total. Rewards can be negotiated for the points remaining, such as visiting a friend on the weekend (e.g. 10 points), using the telephone (e.g. 5 points per 15 minutes), going to a movie (e.g. 25 points) and so on. Rule-following thus leads to gaining the rewards, and rule-breaking risks losing them.

Many of the guidelines for using behaviour contracts that were described in the previous section (page 44) are still relevant here. You may wish to review them to make sure your contract covers all the important points.

Use a family meeting to discuss what the rules will be, and what the rewards will be for following them.

▦ exercise 9 how to use a behaviour contract to manage problem behaviour

Identify a few family rules that your teenager is having difficulty following. You may wish to refer back to the section on family rules on pages 57 and 58.

....

....

Choose rewards or privileges that your teenager will enjoy, and that are appropriate for improved rule-following (refer back to page 43 for ideas).

....

....

Finally, link following the rules with the reward or privilege you have agreed with your teenager. Remember to set moderately easy goals at first so your teenager is rewarded for any improvement, then you can gradually make the goals harder to achieve. See pages 71 to 73 for examples.

....

....

List anything you need to purchase or organise before you can start using the contract.

....

....

Look at the example contract #2A below where Peter is often aggressive with his siblings, there is more yelling than we like, and people often go into other people's rooms without asking. Three rules have been agreed to describe how to behave in these situations: Be gentle, Speak quietly, and Respect privacy.

Peter is keen to go to a weekly football game, to have a family BBQ, and to have some say about what food the family chooses each Friday evening. These are agreed as rewards he can earn.

Next, how will the rewards be obtained? In this example, Peter can earn 3 points per rule per day. With 3 rules, this means that Peter could earn 9 points per day and 63 points per week maximum (3 points × 3 rules × 7 days = 63). However, each instance of rule breaking loses 1 point, and these are deducted from the daily totals.

Rule-following thus leads to access to rewards, and rule-breaking loses them. In this example, there are 3 weekend rewards with different points values. No credit is allowed, which means the rewards are not available if Peter has not earned enough points, although he can carry up to 5 points over to the next week if they are not exchanged for a reward.

example behaviour contract #2a

Between: Peter and Mum/Dad

Starting on: Monday August 9th

Rules:

- Be gentle with each other (no hurting)
- Speak quietly (no yelling)
- Respect privacy and personal space (ask first)

Rewards: Points not lost can be exchanged for privileges. Weekly rewards – go to football game = 30pts; family bbq = 20pts; choose Friday night takeaway food = 10pts

Conditions: No credit; Max. of 5 points carried over to next week

example monitoring chart # 2a

Name: Peter.   Week beginning: Monday, 9th August

ACTIVITY & DETAILS	CARRY OVER	M	T	W	T	F	S	S	TOTAL
Maximum points/day = 9		9	9	9	9	9	9	9	63
Family rules									
• Be gentle – no hurting		/	/		/		/ /		5
• Speak quietly – no yelling		/ / /	/ /	/	/ /	/		/	10
• Respect privacy – ask first		/	/	/	/	/	/ /	/ /	9
Points lost/day		-5	-4	-2	-4	-2	-4	-3	-24
Points already earned/day		+4	+5	+7	+5	+7	+5	+6	39
Points available		4	9	16	21	28	23	29	
Points used						-10		-20	-30
Carried over	0					18		9	9(5)

The example chart above tracks Peter through his week to see how he went. On Monday, Peter broke the 3 rules on a total of 5 occasions. He could have earned 9 points for the day if he had not broken any rules, but now he only has 4 points – 9 minus 5. The next day, Tuesday, he broke the rules 4 times, and ends up with another 5 points. Added to the points he got on Monday, he now has a total of 9 for the week. On Wednesday he has a good day and only breaks the rules twice, so his weekly tally rises to 16. On Thursday, there are 4 rule violations and the weekly tally rises to 21. Friday sees only 2 rules broken and Peter now has 28 points. He decides to trade in 10 points to allow him to choose the family takeaway meal on Friday night. This leaves him with 18 points. On Saturday he breaks 4 rules, and earns another 5 points bringing his total to 23 – not enough to go to the football game this week, but enough to earn the family BBQ on Sunday. On Sunday he earns another 6 points, exchanges 20 to get the family BBQ, and has 9 left over. He can carry 5 of those over to the following week but loses the other 4.

An examination of Peter's chart for the week reveals that he has broken the 'be gentle' rule on 5 occasions; the 'talk quietly' rule on 10 occasions, and the 'respect privacy' rule on 9 occasions. He earned 39 points out of a possible maximum of 63, which means he broke the rules on 24 occasions. He was able to earn 2 of the 3 rewards available, and was allowed to carry 5 of the extra 9 points over to the next week. In order to get him to improve his rule-following it may be necessary to increase the points needed to earn some of the rewards, or add some different rewards.

It is also important to praise and acknowledge Peter's behaviour when he follows the rules. Over the next week or two his behaviour should then gradually improve. The behaviour contract can then be phased out, using occasional praise and access to activities he likes to keep the improvements going.

Sometimes it may be hard to find weekly rewards, or they may be too far in the future to provide motivation on a daily basis. With weekly rewards, parents sometimes find rule-following early in the week is poor. As the weekend gets closer, teenagers try to improve their behaviour in order to get points for weekend activities, but often fail because they leave it too late. This can cause problems for parents and teenagers and it may be necessary to add opportunities for daily rewards.

In the next example, points are totalled up at 6 p.m. each evening, and points earned may then be exchanged for rewards from a menu of daily rewards. Any points lost for rule-breaking after 6 p.m. are deducted from the following day's allocation. If available points are not used on any evening to obtain rewards, they may be carried over for use on other days, or on the weekend, or even on following weeks.

Some limits are often necessary. For example you might want to specify that no more than one hour of telephone calls may be made on any one evening unless special approval is obtained from parents in advance. Or, if there are any more than six rule-breaking events (over 50%) on any day, no rewards may be enjoyed that evening and points are carried over for use on the following evening.

example behaviour contract #2b

Between: Peter and Mum/Dad

Starting on: Monday 9th August

Rules:

- Be gentle with each other (no hurting)
- Speak quietly (no yelling)
- Respect privacy and personal space (ask first)

Rewards: Points not lost can be exchanged for privileges. Daily rewards – 15 minutes telephone time = 2pts; 15 minutes later to bed = 2pts; 15 minutes playing a card game with parent = 2pts; ice cream for dessert = 2pts.

Conditions: No credit; Max. of 5 points carried over to next week. Points are tallied at 6 p.m. each evening; any points lost after 6 p.m. are deducted from next day's total; points may be carried over to the next day, but there is a 60 minute daily maximum on phone calls, card games, or staying up late; if more than 6 rule-breaks occur on any day (6 p.m. to 6 p.m.), all points are frozen and cannot be used that day, although they can be carried over to the next day.

There is no difference in the way the monitoring chart is set up except that the daily points are used to decide whether daily rewards have been earned. In some cases, you might agree that your teenager can choose between having points count towards daily or weekly rewards or both. Several different arrangements are possible.

Discuss any proposed behaviour contract with your teenager and anyone else who might be affected. Make sure you take your draft behaviour contract to a family meeting to discuss how it might work, and to see if it can be improved.

family meeting

Plan another family meeting to discuss what family rules you might want to agree on, and to plan the behaviour contract.

Will you keep to the same time you set for last week's meeting? If not, think about what might be a better time. What else could you do to improve the running of the meeting?

....

....

....

....

summary

This week, six strategies for managing teenagers' problem behaviour were introduced. These included:

- clear family rules
- directed discussion
- clear, calm requests
- logical consequences
- dealing with teenagers' emotions
- behaviour contracts

Think about which of these strategies you would like to use with your teenager.

practice tasks

- Choose one or two strategies introduced in this session (other than the behaviour contract) for managing problem behaviour that you would like to try out with your teenager. Write down the two strategies you plan to use over the next 7 days.

....

....

....

....

- Keep track of how you go by using the checklist on page 76 (an additional copy of this form is provided in the Worksheets section).

- Hold a family meeting to review and revise behaviour contract #1 for increasing teenager behaviour (chores) you designed in Week 2. An example agenda for the family meeting is provided on page 77. Also, you may wish to discuss the family rules you plan to introduce and behaviour contract #2 with your teenager and other family members (use the blank form on page 78). Implement any new contract after you and your teenager have both signed it and set up a new monitoring chart

- Continue monitoring the problem behaviours you selected earlier.

  For a review of the material covered in this section, you may like to watch:

- *Every Parent's Guide to Teenagers*, Part 4, Managing Problem Behaviour.

content of next week

During Week 4 you will be encouraged to practise using some of the positive parenting strategies introduced in Weeks 2 and 3. You will be prompted to track your use of the strategies, identify your strengths and areas for further practice, and set goals for change.

checklist for managing problem behaviour

Choose two of the strategies discussed in Week 3 which you would like to practice with your teenager over the next week. Be as specific as possible (e.g. one goal may be to make clear calm requests with your teenager at least once per day). Use the table below to record whether you reached your goals each day. Comment on what went well and list any problems that occurred.

GOAL 1:

....

....

GOAL 2:

....

....

DAY	GOAL 1 Y/N	GOAL 2 Y/N	COMMENTS
1			
2			
3			
4			
5			
6			
7			

example agenda for family meeting

Preparation

- agree on time and place for meeting; agree on realistic time-limit (e.g. 30 minutes)
- gather all relevant material together from noticeboard
- appoint chairperson, timekeeper, & recorder

Agenda

- *item 1:* discuss Behaviour Contract #1 — Increasing teenager behaviour (chores)
- *item 2:* discuss and negotiate draft Behaviour Contract #2 — Family rules that teenager might agree to
- *item 3:* draw up Monitoring Chart #2
- *item 4:* any other business
- *item 5:* set time for next meeting

Before closing the meeting, quickly review any important decisions that have been made.

Afterwards

Where possible, organise some brief pleasant activity for all family members to do together to reward everyone for taking part in the family meeting.

behaviour contract #2

Between: .... and: ....

Starting on: .... (date) ....

Behaviour/chore: ....

....

....

Reward: ....

....

....

Conditions: ....

....

....

monitoring chart #2

Name: .... Week beginning: ....

ACTIVITY & DETAILS	CARRY OVER	M	T	W	T	F	S	S	TOTAL
Maximum points/day =									
Family rules									
•									
•									
•									
•									
•									
Points lost per day									
Points earned per day									
Points available									
Points used									
Points remaining/carried									

using positive parenting strategies 1

overview

This week is the first of three weeks of practice at using and refining the strategies introduced in Weeks 2 and 3. Each week you will be prompted to practise using these strategies with your teenager and reflect on how well they are working. Aim to set yourself some specific goals. You may find it helpful to keep track of how well you carry out these strategies on the checklists provided. Guidelines for giving yourself some constructive feedback will be introduced. The aim is to identify at least two things you did well during your practice and one or two things you would do differently. The things you identify as areas for change will become your goals for the rest of the week. You may be tempted to miss one or more of these practice weeks and move on to Week 7 — Dealing with Risky Behaviour. This can work for some parents. However, it is important to recognise that the ideas introduced during Weeks 2 and 3 are further developed in Weeks 7 and 8. You may therefore find it difficult to make progress with your teenager's risky behaviour outside your home if you have not first become confident by practising the use of these new ideas at home.

By the end of Week 4 you should be able to:

- Use positive parenting strategies effectively with your teenager.

- Monitor your use of positive parenting strategies.
- Identify your strengths and areas for further practice in using positive parenting strategies.
- Set specific goals for further practice.

review of progress

exercise 1 review use of strategies and routines

What were your practice tasks from last week (refer to page 75)?

....

....

....

What worked? Please be specific and think of at least two positive points. It may be helpful to look at your checklist for managing problem behaviour (page 76).

....

....

....

Is there anything that you could have done differently? You may notice some steps on your checklist that you missed or could improve.

....

....

....

What might you need to practise further?

....

....

....

monitoring your use of the positive parenting strategies

This part of the program aims to help you reflect on how well you are able to use the positive parenting strategies and to remind you of the steps in the strategies you are using. You have now been using several of the strategies introduced during Weeks 2 and 3. You may also be using a behaviour contract to improve your teenager's desirable behaviour or to reduce their undesirable behaviour. You also probably have several clear goals for your teenager and yourself that you are working towards. You may now be noticing that you are combining several of these strategies for particular situations when you have to manage your teenager's behaviour. Select a particular day or time when you think you will have an opportunity to practise using the strategies you have chosen. This will be a time when you and your teenager are together and when you expect to be able to meet the goals you have set yourself. Continue to keep a record of how well you are meeting your goals by completing the practice task checklist on page 85. This will help you identify things that you are doing well and things that are not working so well. An example of a completed practice task checklist appears on page 84. The parent completing this checklist has identified areas that need further improvement. This prompts them to go back and review the steps for these strategies at the relevant sections in Weeks 2 and 3. An additional copy of the Practice Task Checklist is included in the Worksheets section. You may like to keep the checklist handy to refer to during the week to help you remember the steps.

■ exercise 2 keeping track of what you do

You may find it helpful to use the Practice Task Checklist and the checklists on the following pages to remind yourself of the steps to follow when dealing with some common problem behaviours. You can also refer to them later in the week to see how well you went and any steps you may have forgotten or need to practise. This can help you set goals for change. You can also use the checklists at other times if any of these problem behaviours occur. Extra copies of these checklists are included in the Worksheets section.

example practice task checklist

Day: Thursday   Time: between 6 p.m. and 9 p.m.

Note down your goals for this week's practice task/s. Be as specific as possible (e.g. one goal may be to use descriptive praise statements with your teenager at least three times). Use the table below to record whether you reach your goals or not. Comment on what went well and list any problems that occurred.

GOAL 1: Make clear calm requests and use praise for cooperation with requests.

GOAL 2: If my requests are ignored, back up with a logical consequence.

GOAL 3: Coach problem solving to encourage my teenager to be more independent.

	GOALS ACHIEVED Y/N	COMMENTS
GOAL 1:	Y	Requests were fairly specific. Didn't always make praise specific enough.
GOAL 2:	Y	Used logical consequences once. Hard to think fast enough.
GOAL 3:	N	No opportunity.

practice task checklist

Day:...

Time: between .... and ....

Note down your goals for this week's practice task/s. Be as specific as possible (e.g. one goal may be to use logical consequences with your teenager when they don't cooperate with your requests). Use the table below to record whether you reach your goals or not. Comment on what went well and list any problems that occurred. If there is no opportunity to practise a task on the selected day, pick another day later in the week and try again.

GOAL 1:

....

....

GOAL 2:

....

....

GOAL 3:

....

....

	GOALS ACHIEVED Y/N	COMMENTS
GOAL 1:		
GOAL 2:		
GOAL 3:		

checklist for managing whining or complaining

Instructions: Whenever whining or complaining occurs, record Yes, No or NA (not applicable) for each of the steps below.

STEPS TO FOLLOW	DAY / STEPS COMPLETED?						
1. Gain your teenager's attention — use their name.							
2. Make a calm request for your teenager to stop whining or complaining and tell them what to do instead — *Please stop complaining about having to clean your room. Please get on with it quietly.*							
3. Praise them if they do as you request — *Thank you for quietly getting on with cleaning your room.*							
4. If the problem continues, tell your teenager what they have done wrong — *You are still complaining and not cleaning your room. You will now not be able to watch TV until half an hour after you finish.* Do not argue or debate the point.							
5. If your teenager argues or abuses you, tell them the consequence has now increased — *You are continuing to whine and complain — you are now not allowed to watch TV until one hour after you have finished.*							
6. If your teenager becomes abusive, use the routine for dealing with emotional behaviour. However, do not reduce the consequence you have applied.							
7. When the complaining stops and the chore has been completed, allow access to the activity (e.g. watching TV) as promised.							
8. As soon as possible, praise your teenager for doing something without whining or complaining — See Step 3.							
NUMBER OF STEPS COMPLETED:							

checklist for managing fighting or not sharing

Instructions: Whenever fighting, or not sharing or taking turns with others occurs, record Yes, No or NA (not applicable) for each of the steps below.

STEPS TO FOLLOW	DAY						
	STEPS COMPLETED?						
1. Gain your teenager's attention — use their name.							
2. Firmly ask your teenager to stop fighting or arguing and tell them what to do instead — *Please stop fighting over the TV remote control. Work out how you can share it.*							
3. Praise them if they do as you request — *It's great to see you two working out a solution so well.*							
4. If the problem continues, tell your teenager what they have done wrong and the logical consequence — *You are not taking turns as I asked. I'm turning the TV off and taking away the remote control for ten minutes.* Do not argue or debate the point.							
5. If your teenager protests or complains, use the routine for dealing with emotional behaviour.							
6. When the time is up, return the activity as promised.							
7. As soon as possible, praise your teenager for sharing and taking turns — See Step 3.							
8. If the problem happens again, repeat the logical consequences for a longer period. Prompt them to problem solve to come up with a better solution. Help them get started if appropriate, but do not solve it for them.							
NUMBER OF STEPS COMPLETED:							

week 4

checklist for managing rudeness, swearing or disobedience

Instructions: Whenever rudeness, swearing or disobedience occurs, record Yes, No or NA (not applicable) for each of the steps below.

STEPS TO FOLLOW	DAY						
	STEPS COMPLETED?						
1. Gain your teenager's attention — use their name.							
2. Firmly ask your teenager to stop what they are doing and tell them what to do instead — *Please stop swearing at me. Speak to me politely.*							
3. Praise them if they do as you request — *Thank you. I really appreciate it when you speak politely to me.*							
4. If the problem continues, tell your teenager what they have done wrong — *You are not speaking politely* — and the consequence — *You are not permitted to use the phone for the next hour.* Do not argue or debate the point.							
5. If your teenager argues or abuses you, tell them the consequence has now increased — *You are continuing to be rude — you are not allowed to use the phone at all tonight now.*							
6. If necessary, use the routine for dealing with emotional behaviour — go away and do something else until everyone calms down.							
7. The next time your teenager speaks politely, praise them, but do not reduce the consequence — See Step 3.							
NUMBER OF STEPS COMPLETED:							

week 4

checklist for managing emotional behaviour

Instructions: Whenever emotional outbursts occur, record Yes, No or NA (not applicable) for each of the steps below.

STEPS TO FOLLOW	DAY						
	STEPS COMPLETED?						
1. Stop what you are doing and listen to what your teenager is saying — look at their face.							
2. When they have finished, reflect back what you think they are saying — *So what I hear you saying is you think I'm being unfair? Is that it?*							
3. Acknowledge that they are upset or angry — *Well I can see you're really angry about that.*							
4. Stay calm and allow them to explain why they are angry, but do not try to solve the problem or change your decision. Do not debate or argue the point — just listen.							
5. If your teenager calms down enough to talk, ask if there is anything you can do — *Is there any way I can help?*							
6. If your teenager is still angry or rejects your offer, suggest a cooling off period for you both — then go away for a set time and do something else until you both calm down — *I don't think it is helpful to discuss this while you (and I) are feeling angry — Let's talk again in half an hour's time. I'm going outside in the yard until then.*							
7. If your teenager accepts your offer of help, then or later, coach them to problem solve — *Well, what do you want to happen now?*							
8. Praise your teenager for dealing appropriately with their emotions — *I really liked the way you were able to calm down and discuss this with me.*							
NUMBER OF STEPS COMPLETED:							

week 4

checklist for revising a behaviour contract

Instructions: Whenever you believe it is necessary to revise a behaviour contract, record Yes, No or NA (not applicable) for each of the steps below.

STEPS TO FOLLOW	DAY						
	STEPS COMPLETED?						
1. Call a family meeting at a time when both you and your teenager can be present.							
2. Praise your teenager for any improvements that have occurred — *It's great to see that you've been spending more time on your homework since the contract started.*							
3. Explain why you think a change is necessary — *Even though there has been an improvement your homework is still less than it ought to be* or *Now that we've got your homework up, I'd like to talk to you about helping with the washing.*							
4. Discuss exactly what your goal is for the increase in behaviour — *I really want you to get your homework up to at least one hour each night* or *I want you to put your dirty clothes into the basket every night before you go to bed.*							
5. Make an offer or ask your teenager what extra rewards or privileges they think would be appropriate to help get the change established — *I would be willing to let you stay up until 9.30 p.m. on weeknights if you complete one hour of homework before 6 p.m.* or *Perhaps I could buy you a new cap if you were able to put your clothes in the wash every night for two weeks.*							
6. Be prepared to negotiate something that both you and your teenager think is fair and reasonable. Do not agree to something that is one-sided. If you cannot agree and your teenager already gets access to everything they want, consider restricting access to something they are already getting — *OK since you can't come up with anything reasonable, you now have to earn use of the telephone in the evening. You can only use the phone after you have put your clothes in the wash/completed your homework.*							
7. Set up a new monitoring chart, state when the new contract will begin, and thank your teenager for discussing it with you. Arrange another family meeting for a week's time to review how it is going.							
NUMBER OF STEPS COMPLETED:							

week 4

reviewing your practice tasks

Once you have completed your practice tasks, spend some time thinking about what you did well and anything you could do differently next time. Use your completed checklists to help guide you through Exercise 3.

■ exercise 3 reviewing the practice tasks

What do you think you did well during your weekly practice task/s? Aim to identify at least two things you did well (e.g. *I used descriptive praise three times, and I stayed calm when I had to deal with an emotional outburst*). Refer to your goals listed on page 83. Which goals did you achieve?

....

....

....

....

....

....

....

What do you think you could have done differently to improve on your practice task/s? Be specific and think of one or two things you would do differently if you repeated this practice task (e.g. *I need to be more specific when using descriptive praise and say exactly what Jamie did that pleased me, and I need to stop trying to jump into problem solving when Lisa is still angry*). Think about the goals you set on page 83. Was there a goal that you did not reach?

....

....

....

....

....

....

....

You may like to use the space below to make notes about any other issues that arose during the practice tasks that you need to practise further for the remainder of the week.

....

....

....

....

....

....

....

summary

This week you had a chance to practise using some specific positive parenting strategies. You were also able to track your use of the strategies, identify your strengths and areas for further improvement, and set goals for change.

practice tasks

- Make a note of the skills you would like to practise further. Be specific and relate your goals to your practice tasks (e.g. *I'll be more specific when using descriptive praise and say exactly what Jamie did that pleased me, and I'll stop trying to jump into problem-solving when Lisa is still angry.*)

....

....

....

....

....

....

- Hold another family meeting to review progress.
- Continue to keep track of your teenager's behaviour. At this point you need to decide whether to continue monitoring the same behaviour. Use your behaviour graph to aid your decision. A useful guide is to stop monitoring once the behaviour has reached a satisfactory level and maintained at that level for at least five consecutive days. You may then wish to begin monitoring another target behaviour.

For a review of the positive parenting strategies you may like to watch:

- *Every Parent's Guide to Teenagers,* Part 3, Encouraging Appropriate Behaviour.
- *Every Parent's Guide to Teenagers*, Part 4, Managing Problem Behaviour.

content of next week

Next week you will have another opportunity to track your use of the positive parenting strategies. You will again be prompted to identify your strengths and areas for further improvement, and set goals for change.

using positive parenting strategies 2

overview

This week gives you another opportunity to practise using and refining the strategies introduced in Weeks 2 and 3. Once again you will be prompted to practise using these strategies with your teenager and reflect on how well they are working. Alternatively, you may decide that things are going really well and you prefer to move on to Week 7 – Dealing with Risky Behaviour. However, if things are not going as well as you had hoped, you might find it more valuable to complete Week 5 first. Before moving to Week 7 it is expected that you will be using logical consequences, problem solving, dealing with emotional behaviour, and using behaviour contracts effectively at home. The goals for this week's practice will often be related to the skills you set yourself to practise after your last practice session. Again you will be prompted to keep track of how well you carry out these strategies on the checklists provided. You will be prompted once more to identify your strengths and areas for further practice, and set new goals for change.

By the end of Week 5 you should be able to:

- Use positive parenting strategies effectively with your teenager.
- Monitor your use of positive parenting strategies.

- Identify your strengths and areas for further practice in using positive parenting strategies.
- Set specific goals for further practice.

review of progress

▨ exercise 1 review use of strategies and routines

What were your practice tasks from last week (refer to page 90)?

....

....

....

What worked? Please be specific and think of at least two positive points. It may be helpful to look at your checklists on pages 83 to 86.

....

....

....

Is there anything that you could have done differently? You may notice some steps on your checklist/s that you missed or could improve.

....

....

....

What might you need to practise further (refer to page 90)?

....

....

....

monitoring your use of the positive parenting strategies

This part of the program aims to help you reflect on how well you are able to use the positive parenting strategies and to remind you of the steps in the strategies you are using. You have now been using several of the strategies introduced during Weeks 2 and 3. You may also be using a behaviour contract to improve your teenager's desirable behaviour or to reduce their undesirable behaviour. You also probably have several clear goals for your teenager and yourself that you are working towards. You may now be noticing that you are combining several of these strategies for particular situations when you have to manage your teenager's behaviour. Select a particular day or time when you think you will have an opportunity to practise using the strategies you have chosen. This will be a time when you and your teenager are together and when you expect to be able to meet the goals you have set yourself. Continue to keep a record of how well you are meeting your goals by completing the practice task checklist on page 98. An additional copy of this form is included in the Worksheets section. You may like to keep the checklist handy to refer to during the week to help you remember the steps.

■ exercise 2 keeping track of what you do

You may find it helpful to use the Practice Task Checklist and the checklists on the following pages to remind yourself of the steps to follow when dealing with some common problem behaviours. You can also refer to them later in the week to see how well you went and any steps you may have forgotten or need to practise. This can help you set goals for change. You can also use the checklists at other times if any of these problem behaviours occur. Extra copies of these checklists are included in the Worksheets section.

practice task checklist

Day:..

Time: between .... and ....

Note down your goals for this week's practice task/s. Be as specific as possible (e.g. one goal may be to use logical consequences with your teenager when they don't cooperate with your requests). Use the table below to record whether you reach your goals or not. Comment on what went well and list any problems that occurred. If there is no opportunity to practise a task on the selected day, pick another day later in the week and try again.

GOAL 1:

....

....

GOAL 2:

....

....

GOAL 3:

....

....

	GOALS ACHIEVED Y/N	COMMENTS
GOAL 1:		
GOAL 2:		
GOAL 3:		

checklist for managing whining or complaining

Instructions: Whenever whining or complaining occurs, record Yes, No or NA (not applicable) for each of the steps below.

STEPS TO FOLLOW	DAY						
	STEPS COMPLETED?						
1. Gain your teenager's attention — use their name.							
2. Make a calm request for your teenager to stop whining or complaining and tell them what to do instead — *Please stop complaining about having to clean your room. Please get on with it quietly.*							
3. Praise them if they do as you request — *Thank you for quietly getting on with cleaning your room.*							
4. If the problem continues, tell your teenager what they have done wrong — *You are still complaining and not cleaning your room. You will now not be able to watch TV until half an hour after you finish.* Do not argue or debate the point.							
5. If your teenager argues or abuses you, tell them the consequence has now increased — *You are continuing to whine and complain — you are now not allowed to watch TV until one hour after you have finished.*							
6. If your teenager becomes abusive, use the routine for dealing with emotional behaviour. However, do not reduce the consequence you have applied.							
7. When the complaining stops and the chore has been completed, allow access to the activity (e.g. watching TV) as promised.							
8. As soon as possible, praise your teenager for doing something without whining or complaining — See Step 3.							
NUMBER OF STEPS COMPLETED:							

checklist for managing fighting or not sharing

Instructions: Whenever fighting, or not sharing or taking turns with others occurs, record Yes, No or NA (not applicable) for each of the steps below.

STEPS TO FOLLOW	DAY	STEPS COMPLETED?							
1. Gain your teenager's attention — use their name.									
2. Firmly ask your teenager to stop fighting or arguing and tell them what to do instead — *Please stop fighting over the TV remote control. Work out how you can share it.*									
3. Praise them if they do as you request — *It's great to see you two working out a solution so well.*									
4. If the problem continues, tell your teenager what they have done wrong and the logical consequence — *You are not taking turns as I asked. I'm turning the TV off and taking away the remote control for ten minutes.* Do not argue or debate the point.									
5. If your teenager protests or complains, use the routine for dealing with emotional behaviour.									
6. When the time is up, return the activity as promised.									
7. As soon as possible, praise your teenager for sharing and taking turns — See Step 3.									
8. If the problem happens again, repeat the logical consequences for a longer period. Prompt them to problem solve to come up with a better solution. Help them get started if appropriate, but do not solve it for them.									
NUMBER OF STEPS COMPLETED:									

checklist for managing rudeness, swearing or disobedience

Instructions: Whenever rudeness, swearing or disobedience occurs, record Yes, No or NA (not applicable) for each of the steps below.

STEPS TO FOLLOW	DAY						
	STEPS COMPLETED?						
1. Gain your teenager's attention — use their name.							
2. Firmly ask your teenager to stop what they are doing and tell them what to do instead — *Please stop swearing at me. Speak to me politely.*							
3. Praise them if they do as you request — *Thank you. I really appreciate it when you speak politely to me.*							
4. If the problem continues, tell your teenager what they have done wrong — *You are not speaking politely* — and the consequence — *You are not permitted to use the phone for the next hour.* Do not argue or debate the point.							
5. If your teenager argues or abuses you, tell them the consequence has now increased — *You are continuing to be rude — you are not allowed to use the phone at all tonight now.*							
6. If necessary, use the routine for dealing with emotional behaviour — go away and do something else until everyone calms down.							
7. The next time your teenager speaks politely, praise them, but do not reduce the consequence — See Step 3.							
NUMBER OF STEPS COMPLETED:							

week 5

checklist for managing emotional behaviour

Instructions: Whenever emotional outbursts occur, record Yes, No or NA (not applicable) for each of the steps below.

STEPS TO FOLLOW	DAY						
	STEPS COMPLETED?						
1. Stop what you are doing and listen to what your teenager is saying — look at their face.							
2. When they have finished, reflect back what you think they are saying — *So what I hear you saying is you think I'm being unfair? Is that it?*							
3. Acknowledge that they are upset or angry — *Well I can see you're really angry about that.*							
4. Stay calm and allow them to explain why they are angry, but do not try to solve the problem or change your decision. Do not debate or argue the point — just listen.							
5. If your teenager calms down enough to talk, ask if there is anything you can do — *Is there any way I can help?*							
6. If your teenager is still angry or rejects your offer, suggest a cooling off period for you both — then go away for a set time and do something else until you both calm down — *I don't think it is helpful to discuss this while you (and I) are feeling angry — Let's talk again in half an hour's time. I'm going outside in the yard until then.*							
7. If your teenager accepts your offer of help, then or later, coach them to problem solve — *Well, what do you want to happen now?*							
8. Praise your teenager for dealing appropriately with their emotions — *I really liked the way you were able to calm down and discuss this with me.*							
NUMBER OF STEPS COMPLETED:							

week 5

checklist for revising a behaviour contract

Instructions: Whenever you believe it is necessary to revise a behaviour contract, record Yes, No or NA (not applicable) for each of the steps below.

STEPS TO FOLLOW	DAY						
	STEPS COMPLETED?						
1. Call a family meeting at a time when both you and your teenager can be present.							
2. Praise your teenager for any improvements that have occurred — *It's great to see that you've been spending more time on your homework since the contract started.*							
3. Explain why you think a change is necessary — *Even though there has been an improvement your homework is still less than it ought to be* or *Now that we've got your homework up, I'd like to talk to you about helping with the washing.*							
4. Discuss exactly what your goal is for the increase in behaviour — *I really want you to get your homework up to at least one hour each night* or *I want you to put your dirty clothes into the basket every night before you go to bed.*							
5. Make an offer or ask your teenager what extra rewards or privileges they think would be appropriate to help get the change established — *I would be willing to let you stay up until 9.30 p.m. on weeknights if you complete one hour of homework before 6 p.m.* or *Perhaps I could buy you a new cap if you were able to put your clothes in the wash every night for two weeks.*							
6. Be prepared to negotiate something that both you and your teenager think is fair and reasonable. Do not agree to something that is one-sided. If you cannot agree and your teenager already gets access to everything they want, consider restricting access to something they are already getting — *OK since you can't come up with anything reasonable, you now have to earn use of the telephone in the evening. You can only use the phone after you have put your clothes in the wash/completed your homework.*							
7. Set up a new monitoring chart, state when the new contract will begin, and thank your teenager for discussing it with you. Arrange another family meeting for a week's time to review how it is going.							
NUMBER OF STEPS COMPLETED:							

week 5

reviewing your practice tasks

Once you have completed your practice tasks, spend some time thinking about what you did well and anything you could do differently next time. Use your completed checklists to help guide you through Exercise 3.

■ exercise 3 reviewing the practice tasks

What do you think you did well during your weekly practice task/s? Aim to identify at least two things you did well (e.g. *I showed affection to my teenager at least once each day, and I made clear, calm requests when I needed cooperation.*) Refer to your goals listed on page 96. Which goals did you achieve?

....

....

....

....

....

....

....

What do you think you could have done differently to improve on your practice task/s? Be specific and think of one or two things you would do differently if you repeated this practice task (e.g. *I need to be more careful not to embarrass Lisa, and I need to time my requests better*). Think about the goals you set on page 96. Was there a goal that you did not reach?

....

....

....

....

....

....

....

You may like to use the space below to make notes about any other issues that arose during the practice tasks that you need to practise further for the remainder of the week.

....

....

....

....

....

....

....

summary

This week you had a chance to practise using some specific positive parenting strategies. You were also able to track your use of the strategies, identify your strengths and areas for further improvement, and set goals for change.

practice tasks

- Make a note of the skills you would like to practise further. Be specific and relate your goals to your practice tasks (e.g. *I'll be more careful not to embarrass Lisa when showing affection, and I'll time my requests better*).

....

....

....

....

....

....

- Hold another family meeting to review progress.
- Continue to keep track of your teenager's behaviour. At this point you need to decide whether to continue monitoring the same behaviour. Use your behaviour graph to aid your decision. A useful guide is to stop monitoring once the behaviour has reached a satisfactory level and maintained at that level for at least five consecutive days. You may then wish to begin monitoring another target behaviour.

For a review of the positive parenting strategies you may like to watch:

- *Every Parent's Guide to Teenagers*, Part 3, Encouraging Appropriate Behaviour.
- *Every Parent's Guide to Teenagers*, Part 4, Managing Problem Behaviour.

content of next week

Next week you will have a further opportunity to track your use of the positive parenting strategies. You will again be prompted to identify your strengths and areas for further improvement, and set goals for change.

using positive parenting strategies 3

This is the third and final week of setting up opportunities to practise using and refining the strategies introduced in Weeks 2 and 3. Once again you will be prompted to practise using these strategies with your teenager and reflect on how well they are working. As before, the goals for this week's practice will often be related to the skills you set yourself to practise after your last practice session. Again you will be prompted to keep track of how well you carry out these strategies on the checklists provided. You will be prompted once more to identify your strengths and areas for further improvement, and set new goals for change. Before moving on to Week 7, it is expected that you will be using logical consequences, problem solving, dealing with emotional behaviour, and using behaviour contracts effectively at home. If you think these strategies are not working after Week 6, continue for one more week or seek professional help.

By the end of Week 6 you should be able to:

- Use positive parenting strategies effectively with your teenager.
- Monitor your use of positive parenting strategies.
- Identify your strengths and areas for further improvement in using positive parenting strategies.
- Set specific goals for further practice where necessary.

review of progress

■ exercise 1 review use of strategies and routines

What were your practice tasks from last week (refer to page 102)?

....

....

....

What worked? Please be specific and think of at least two positive points. It may be helpful to look at your checklists on pages 96 to 101.

....

....

....

Is there anything that you could have done differently? You may notice some steps on your checklist/s that you missed or could improve.

....

....

....

What might you need to practise further (refer to page 103)?

....

....

....

week 6

monitoring your use of the positive parenting strategies

This part of the program aims to help you reflect on how well you are able to use the positive parenting strategies and to remind you of the steps in the strategies you are using. You have now been using several of the strategies introduced during Weeks 2 and 3. You may also be using a behaviour contract to improve your teenager's desirable behaviour or to reduce their undesirable behaviour. You also probably have several clear goals for your teenager and yourself that you are working towards. You may now be noticing that you are combining several of these strategies for particular situations when you have to manage your teenager's behaviour. Select a particular day or time when you think you will have an opportunity to practise using the strategies you have chosen. This will be a time when you and your teenager are together and when you expect to be able to meet the goals you have set yourself. Continue to keep a record of how well you are meeting your goals by completing the practice task checklist on page 110. An additional copy of this form is included in the Worksheets section. You may like to keep the checklist handy to refer to during the week to help you remember the steps.

■ exercise 2 keeping track of what you do

You may find it helpful to use the Practice Task Checklist and the checklists on the following pages to remind yourself of the steps to follow when dealing with some common problem behaviours. You can also refer to them later in the week to see how well you went and any steps you may have forgotten or need to practise. This can help you set goals for change. You can also use the checklists at other times if any of these problem behaviours occur. Extra copies of these checklists are included in the Worksheets section.

practice task checklist

Day: ....

Time: between .... and ....

Note down your goals for this week's practice task/s. Be as specific as possible (e.g. one goal may be to use logical consequences with your teenager when they don't cooperate with your requests). Use the table below to record whether you reach your goals or not. Comment on what went well and list any problems that occurred. If there is no opportunity to practise a task on the selected day, pick another day later in the week and try again.

GOAL 1:

....

....

GOAL 2:

....

....

GOAL 3:

....

....

	GOALS ACHIEVED Y/N	COMMENTS
GOAL 1:		
GOAL 2:		
GOAL 3:		

week 6

checklist for managing whining or complaining

Instructions: Whenever whining or complaining occurs, record Yes, No or NA (not applicable) for each of the steps below.

STEPS TO FOLLOW	DAY						
	STEPS COMPLETED?						
1. Gain your teenager's attention — use their name.							
2. Make a calm request for your teenager to stop whining or complaining and tell them what to do instead — *Please stop complaining about having to clean your room. Please get on with it quietly.*							
3. Praise them if they do as you request — *Thank you for quietly getting on with cleaning your room.*							
4. If the problem continues, tell your teenager what they have done wrong — *You are still complaining and not cleaning your room. You will now not be able to watch TV until half an hour after you finish.* Do not argue or debate the point.							
5. If your teenager argues or abuses you, tell them the consequence has now increased — *You are continuing to whine and complain — you are now not allowed to watch TV until one hour after you have finished.*							
6. If your teenager becomes abusive, use the routine for dealing with emotional behaviour. However, do not reduce the consequence you have applied.							
7. When the complaining stops and the chore has been completed, allow access to the activity (e.g. watching TV) as promised.							
8. As soon as possible, praise your teenager for doing something without whining or complaining — See Step 3.							
NUMBER OF STEPS COMPLETED:							

week 6

checklist for managing fighting or not sharing

Instructions: Whenever fighting, or not sharing or taking turns with others occurs, record Yes, No or NA (not applicable) for each of the steps below.

STEPS TO FOLLOW	DAY							
	STEPS COMPLETED?							
1. Gain your teenager's attention — use their name.								
2. Firmly ask your teenager to stop fighting or arguing and tell them what to do instead — *Please stop fighting over the TV remote control. Work out how you can share it.*								
3. Praise them if they do as you request — *It's great to see you two working out a solution so well.*								
4. If the problem continues, tell your teenager what they have done wrong and the logical consequence — *You are not taking turns as I asked. I'm turning the TV off and taking away the remote control for ten minutes.* Do not argue or debate the point.								
5. If your teenager protests or complains, use the routine for dealing with emotional behaviour.								
6. When the time is up, return the activity as promised.								
7. As soon as possible, praise your teenager for sharing and taking turns — See Step 3.								
8. If the problem happens again, repeat the logical consequences for a longer period. Prompt them to problem solve to come up with a better solution. Help them get started if appropriate, but do not solve it for them.								
NUMBER OF STEPS COMPLETED:								

week 6

checklist for managing rudeness, swearing or disobedience

Instructions: Whenever rudeness, swearing or disobedience occurs, record Yes, No or NA (not applicable) for each of the steps below.

STEPS TO FOLLOW	DAY						
	STEPS COMPLETED?						
1. Gain your teenager's attention — use their name.							
2. Firmly ask your teenager to stop what they are doing and tell them what to do instead — *Please stop swearing at me. Speak to me politely.*							
3. Praise them if they do as you request — *Thank you. I really appreciate it when you speak politely to me.*							
4. If the problem continues, tell your teenager what they have done wrong — *You are not speaking politely* — and the consequence — *You are not permitted to use the phone for the next hour.* Do not argue or debate the point.							
5. If your teenager argues or abuses you, tell them the consequence has now increased — *You are continuing to be rude — you are not allowed to use the phone at all tonight now.*							
6. If necessary, use the routine for dealing with emotional behaviour — go away and do something else until everyone calms down.							
7. The next time your teenager speaks politely, praise them, but do not reduce the consequence — See Step 3.							
NUMBER OF STEPS COMPLETED:							

week 6

checklist for managing emotional behaviour

Instructions: Whenever emotional outbursts occur, record Yes, No or NA (not applicable) for each of the steps below.

STEPS TO FOLLOW	DAY STEPS COMPLETED?						
1. Stop what you are doing and listen to what your teenager is saying — look at their face.							
2. When they have finished, reflect back what you think they are saying — *So what I hear you saying is you think I'm being unfair? Is that it?*							
3. Acknowledge that they are upset or angry — *Well I can see you're really angry about that.*							
4. Stay calm and allow them to explain why they are angry, but do not try to solve the problem or change your decision. Do not debate or argue the point — just listen.							
5. If your teenager calms down enough to talk, ask if there is anything you can do — *Is there any way I can help?*							
6. If your teenager is still angry or rejects your offer, suggest a cooling off period for you both — then go away for a set time and do something else until you both calm down — *I don't think it is helpful to discuss this while you (and I) are feeling angry — Let's talk again in half an hour's time. I'm going outside in the yard until then.*							
7. If your teenager accepts your offer of help, then or later, coach them to problem solve — *Well, what do you want to happen now?*							
8. Praise your teenager for dealing appropriately with their emotions — *I really liked the way you were able to calm down and discuss this with me.*							
NUMBER OF STEPS COMPLETED:							

checklist for revising a behaviour contract

Instructions: Whenever you believe it is necessary to revise a behaviour contract, record Yes, No or NA (not applicable) for each of the steps below.

	DAY						
STEPS TO FOLLOW	STEPS COMPLETED?						
1. Call a family meeting at a time when both you and your teenager can be present.							
2. Praise your teenager for any improvements that have occurred — *It's great to see that you've been coming home on time more often since the contract started.*							
3. Explain why you think a change is necessary — *Even though there has been an improvement you are still late sometimes* or *Now that you are coming home on time, I'd like to talk to you about helping with the cleaning.*							
4. Discuss exactly what your goal is for the increase in behaviour — *I really want you to be home on time every day* or *I want you to clean up your room every morning before you go to school.*							
5. Make an offer or ask your teenager what extra rewards or privileges they think would be appropriate to help get the change established — *I would be willing to let you stay out until 11 p.m. on Friday nights if you come home on time every day this week*, or *Perhaps I could buy you a new magazine if you were able to clean your room every morning this week.*							
6. Be prepared to negotiate something that both you and your teenager think is fair and reasonable. Do not agree to something that is one-sided. If you cannot agree and your teenager already gets access to everything they want, consider restricting access to something they are already getting — *OK since you can't come up with anything reasonable, you now have to earn your allowance. You can only have your allowance if you come home on time/ clean up your room.*							
7. Set up a new monitoring chart, state when the new contract will begin, and thank your teenager for discussing it with you. Arrange another family meeting for a week's time to review how it is going.							
NUMBER OF STEPS COMPLETED:							

week 6

reviewing your practice tasks

Once you have completed your practice tasks, spend some time thinking about what you did well and anything you could do differently next time. Use your completed checklists to help guide you through Exercise 3.

■ exercise 3 reviewing the practice tasks

What do you think you did well during your weekly practice task/s? Aim to identify at least two things you did well (e.g. *I set up a behaviour contract to reduce Adam's swearing and improve his helping with chores, and we held a family meeting to discuss the contract*). Refer to your goals listed on page 108). Which goals did you achieve?

....

....

....

....

....

....

....

What do you think you could have done differently to improve on your practice task/s? Be specific and think of one or two things you would do differently if you repeated this practice task (e.g. *I need to be prepared to let Adam suggest rewards that are valued by him, and I need to stop trying to run the family meeting on my own*). Think about the goals you set on page 108. Was there a goal that you did not reach?

....

....

....

....

....

....

....

....

You may like to use the space below to make notes about any other issues that arose during the practice tasks that you need to practise further for the remainder of the week.

....

....

....

....

....

....

....

....

summary

This week you had another chance to practise using the positive parenting strategies in a structured practice exercise. You were also able to track your use of the strategies, identify your strengths and areas for further improvement, and set goals for change.

practice tasks

- Make a note of the skills you would like to practise further. Be specific and relate your goals to your practice tasks (e.g. *I'll ask Adam to suggest possible rewards for the behaviour contract, and I'll ask other family members to help run the family meetings.*)

....

....

....

....

....

....

- Hold another family meeting to review progress.
- Continue to keep track of your teenager's behaviour. At this point you need to decide whether to continue monitoring the same behaviour. Use your behaviour graph to aid your decision. A useful guide is to stop monitoring once the behaviour has reached a satisfactory level and maintained at that level for at least five consecutive days. You may then wish to begin monitoring another target behaviour.

For a review of the positive parenting strategies you may like to watch:

- *Every Parent's Guide to Teenagers,* Part 3, Encouraging Appropriate Behaviour.
- *Every Parent's Guide to Teenagers*, Part 4, Managing Problem Behaviour.

content of next week

During Week 7 you will look at family survival tips to help make the task of parenting easier. You will also be introduced to a routine called Planning Ahead for Dealing with Risky Behaviour. This will assist you to deal with situations where your teenager might want to engage in activities that might be risky for their health or wellbeing, or their future opportunities.

dealing with risky behaviour

overview

If you have spent the last two or three weeks practising some of the strategies introduced during Weeks 2 and 3, your teenager's behaviour at home should be improving by now. However, as teenagers spend more time with people away from home, they may develop opinions that differ from those of their parents. They may also experiment more and take unacceptable risks. This can lead to conflict at home, especially if parents try and restrict these activities. Discussions on these topics can often become unpleasant and destructive. Parents sometimes try to restrict their teenager's activities, not because of the activity itself, but because of concern and fear about what else might happen to them. Certainly some of these fears are real, but others may be blown out of proportion by the media. The challenge for parents is to help educate their teenager so that they recognise risky situations, avoid them if possible, and escape from those that cannot be avoided. This week, you will also look at family survival tips to help make parenting easier.

By the end of Week 7 you should be able to:

• Identify situations that may put your teenager's health or wellbeing at risk.

- Describe the steps involved in designing a routine to deal with risky behaviour (i.e. plan ahead, talk about concerns and risks, select risk-reduction strategies, use rewards for appropriate behaviour, use back-up consequences for inappropriate behaviour, and hold a follow-up review).
- Construct a community contact network to help monitor your teenager's behaviour.
- Use the family survival tips to help make the task of parenting easier.

review of progress

▓ exercise 1 review use of strategies and routines

What were your practice tasks from last week (refer to page 115)?

....

....

....

What worked? Please be specific and think of at least two positive points. It may be helpful to look at your checklists on pages 108-113.

....

....

....

Is there anything that you could have done differently? You may notice some steps on your checklist/s that you missed or could improve.

....

....

....

What might you need to practise further (refer to page 115)?

....

....

....

risky situations

Some situations pose a risk because your teenager may behave in certain ways in order to obtain the approval of other teenagers. You might be concerned because this may lead to your teenager behaving in ways you do not like. There may also be real risks for your teenager if they are unable to resist the temptation to engage in illegal or antisocial behaviour. For example, you may be concerned if your teenager is hanging around the shops with friends who are known to shoplift. Your teenager may know that they are not supposed to enter a shop with these friends. However, they may decide that 'nothing will happen' and that you will never find out anyway. Parental approval for 'doing the right thing' probably will not compete well with some immediate excitement and the enjoyment of going into the shop with their friends. Children and teenagers usually get into difficulties because of a chain of events. The events at the beginning of a chain often do not seem particularly risky but if parents do not monitor these events, and teenagers are not taught how to manage them, they can quickly lead to more serious situations.

These situations can also be risky because demands by your teenager to take part in these activities might lead you to try to force your teenager to give in to your wishes. This can sometimes lead to serious conflict and resentment. The routine presented here recognises that all strategies have their limitations and no single strategy will work for all situations. Sometimes several strategies are needed in combination and this routine suggests how the ideas considered during the previous weeks can now be combined to deal with these more difficult situations.

■ exercise 2 identifying risky situations

Situation	✓	Comments
• visiting friends	☐	
• going to parties	☐	
• going off with friends (e.g. camping)	☐	
• school holidays	☐	
• going out at night (e.g. movies)	☐	
• weekends	☐	
• on the way to or home from school	☐	
• travelling on public transport	☐	
• going to local stores, shopping centre, etc.	☐	
• after school	☐	
• alone at home	☐	
• other	☐	
	☐	
	☐	

routine for dealing with risky behaviour

Many teenagers are tempted to smoke, drink alcohol, miss school, or join their peers in other risky activities. They may want to drop commitments that are demanding, such as sports training, music practice, or even homework. This is partly because the natural rewards for resisting temptation or persisting with a difficult task are usually delayed. In contrast, the rewards for giving in to temptation are usually immediate and powerful, especially if provided by peers. There can also often be unpleasant consequences for not joining in with their peers, such as social isolation, teasing, and bullying.

These situations create a special challenge. We call them risky situations because they can be more difficult for parents to handle, and the consequences of making a wrong decision can be serious for all concerned.

Putting too many restrictions on your teenager prevents them from developing important skills, and increases the risks when they finally leave your supervision. Some parents believe that the best strategy to prevent their teenager getting into trouble with people, places, or events that might be risky, is to prevent them from having contact with them. This can work for a while but it often creates other problems. You cannot protect your teenager from temptation forever. Sooner or later they will leave home, and if they have not had practice dealing with these issues, they are more likely to get into trouble. By keeping your teenager away from these situations, you deny them the opportunity to learn how to handle temptation. Although they might be avoiding risky situations because of your restrictions, they are also probably missing out on a lot of other positive experiences that could be valuable or enjoyable.

Severely restricting your teenager often causes growing resentment. You may find you are having more and more arguments and conflicts about your attempts to enforce your restrictions. Alternatively, you may find your teenager increasingly withdrawn or sullen, spending lots of time in his or her room, and perhaps refusing to talk or eat. These are danger signals that tell you the effects of your strategy of restriction may be costing more than it is worth.

You have a wealth of knowledge from your own experiences, and this could be used to help your teenager learn the best way to avoid risky situations.

Planning ahead for risky situations can avoid many problems. The recommended routine involves problem solving ahead of time to prevent serious problems from occurring. The main idea is to anticipate risky activities that your teenager may wish to be involved in. By being clear about what you want your teenager to do to reduce or avoid risk, you can prevent most problems from occurring.

The routine for dealing with risky behaviour requires you to follow these steps:

identify risky situations

If you can do this in advance, you avoid being put under pressure to make a decision without having time to think through the details. Often talking to other parents or older teenagers will help you anticipate difficult times ahead. Going to sleep-overs, parties and late-night movies; driving around with older teenagers; or hanging out at the shopping centre are a few situations where teenagers can be exposed to risk and temptation. Think about what your teenager is likely to want to go to and what your response is going to be. You do not want them being exposed to risks they cannot manage, but nor do you want to prevent them from having fun with their friends.

do some advance planning

Decide whether you need to obtain information before you sit down to talk with your teenager. You may want to find out about public transport, movie locations and screening times, phone cards, taxi company phone numbers, and other parents' phone numbers. Sometimes you will want your teenager to do some of this work – on other occasions it pays to be prepared. You can always get them to obtain the information, even if you know it already! They need to take responsibility for obtaining information about things they want to do. You may have to help them locate information sources – but they should obtain the information themselves if they can.

talk about concerns and risks

Your teenager needs to understand your concerns, and the risks you have identified you want to reduce or avoid. Find a time to talk together when you will not be interrupted. Explain why you are concerned about their going to a late night movie or party (e.g. drugs, sex, alcohol). Use an 'I' statement, such as – *I'm concerned that someone might get you drunk.* This is better than a 'You' statement, such as – *You might get drunk.* 'You' statements invite an argument, such as – *No I won't*, whereas 'I' statements invite your teenager to convince you that they can avoid this situation. Tell them you are willing to allow them to go if you can

week 7

be assured they have a plan to avoid getting into trouble, and that together you want to come up with some rules that they will agree to follow. They may protest that your fears are groundless and you are over-reacting. Unless they can prove to your satisfaction that they are correct, you should insist that it is your concerns that need to be addressed, and you are not prepared to let them attend unless they have a plan you are happy with.

Many teenagers get into trouble because they suddenly find themselves in a situation they had not thought about. It is often very difficult for them to come up with a sensible solution at that time. They need your help to plan ahead so they do not get into risky situations they are not prepared for.

select risk-reduction strategies

Decide on rules for appropriate behaviour in the situation and discuss them calmly with your teenager. These include details such as what time to be home, and what to do if something unexpected happens, like missing the last bus. Problem solve with your teenager to come up with the best plan you can between you. Refer back to the problem solving steps on pages 40 to 42 if necessary. You need to be satisfied that your teenager has a plan to deal with events you are concerned about, even though they may protest that they will never happen. If your teenager protests that it is not worth going under the conditions you impose, point out that if it works out okay this time, you will review it for next time. They can take it or leave it.

After you and your teenager have a plan, make sure it includes what they will say if they are pressured to break the rules. Then, get them to practise with you. It is one thing for your teenager to be able to talk about what they might say, but another thing entirely to actually get the words and the emphasis right. Your teenager will be much more likely to stick to their plan if they practise. If done well, this can be a very effective and enjoyable exercise. Although the situation is a serious one, you and your teenager can have fun trying out different ways of saying the words until they find a way they feel comfortable with.

For your practice, pick a time when there is no one else around and you are not likely to be disturbed. Ask your teenager to describe a situation that might occur during the event or situation you are discussing. Make it as realistic as possible – do not just sit and talk about how to do it. Your teenager needs to practise in a situation that is similar to the real thing.

Get them to describe the place, the time, and the person/s involved so you have a clear picture. It can help if you agree where each person is sitting or standing and literally 'walk' though the scenario. Sometimes having only one response may not be enough. You may need to practise a few different responses so your teenager can choose the one that best suits the situation they are in. In this way you should be able to improve your teenager's skill in using their plan when it is needed.

Immediately before the risky situation occurs, ask your teenager to repeat the rules – *So what did we decide you should do after the movie is over?; What did we decide you would do if the others start smoking dope?*

reward appropriate behaviour

If your teenager sits down with you and works out a satisfactory agreement they should be rewarded by gaining limited access to the activities and events they want to take part in – this way a compromise can be negotiated to satisfy everyone. Sometimes an additional reward for keeping to the plan might be appropriate.

For example, if your teenager reliably comes home on time from the movie on Friday night, they might get to go to another highly desired event, such as an important sporting event or music concert.

specify a back-up consequence

This acts as a deterrent to discourage risky behaviour. This may be necessary because parental approval and other rewards for keeping to the plan can sometimes be overshadowed by those on offer from peers and peer-related activities. For example, imagine your teenager is with friends after a movie. They decide to go to a nearby coffee shop but this will mean missing the bus they agreed to catch. At this point, peer pressure is competing with their agreement with you. For a back-up consequence to be effective as a deterrent it needs to be fairly important to your teenager. It must be something you are willing to impose if you have to – do not pick a consequence you would not ever be able or willing to impose. However, do not pick one that is so severe your teenager might avoid coming home because of it. Often teenagers will be confident that they will follow the rules and will suggest appropriate consequences themselves. Avoid consequences that work against other goals or contracts.

hold a follow-up review session after the event

This allows you both to review how well the plan worked, and to modify it if necessary for next time. In this discussion, which should be held fairly soon after the event, the aim is to praise any successes, and if necessary, briefly and calmly describe any part of the plan that the teenager forgot, or that did not work well. If necessary, return to problem solving to revise the plan for next time a similar event occurs. If you had to impose a consequence because of a failure to follow the agreed plan, discuss how and when your teenager might be allowed to try again. Remember your goal should be to assist your teenager to behave appropriately in risky situations. Preventing them from going to such activities at all does not allow them to learn these skills, and sets up resentment and conflict that can lead to serious family breakdown in the long run.

A sample routine for a young teenage girl wanting to go to a late-night movie on a Friday night is described on page 124. This shows how all the steps fit together to make a routine for dealing with risky behaviour.

example routine for dealing with risky behaviour

Wanting to go to a late-night movie and then a coffee shop afterwards

Identify the risky situation

- Drinking alcohol or using drugs after attending a late-night movie on Friday night

List any advanced planning or preparation

- Check movie screening times
- Check with parents of peers to see if they share your concerns, and what they are planning, if anything — you may be able to combine plans

Talk about concerns and risks

- Friends pressuring teenager to 'join in' or 'just try it'
- Missing last bus home and being at risk of abduction or attack
- Using drugs or alcohol and being taken advantage of sexually

Select risk-reduction strategies

- If her friends choose to go to a bar instead of the coffee shop, she will go to the coffee shop on her own
- If there is no one she knows in the coffee shop, she will come straight home
- She will phone parents from the coffee shop when she arrives
- In any case, she will catch the 11.30 bus and be home by midnight
- She will take change for the phone (or a cell phone), plus the fare for the bus
- She will check the return bus times on her way in, and work out in advance how long it takes to walk from the coffee shop to the bus stop

Agree on a reward for appropriate behaviour

- Praise and approval for any participation in selecting risk-reduction strategies
- Special event on Saturday, perhaps with a parent (e.g. trip to a sporting event or going shopping)
- Points toward a larger more distant reward (e.g. computer game, new clothes)

Specify a back-up consequence for problem behaviour

- Penalty for not keeping to the plan — not permitted to go out at night to social events for the next 2 weeks
- Loss of points toward larger reward
- No special event on Saturday

List information/items required to make the plan work

- Times of buses coming home late on Friday night
- Check out how long it takes to walk from the coffee shop to the bus stop
- Enough money for bus fare and phone call

Hold a follow-up discussion to evaluate how well the plan worked (carried out after the event)

week 7

■ exercise 3 developing a routine for dealing with risky behaviour

Now you have the chance to design your own routine. For this first practise, think of a recent situation that might have or really did put your teenager at risk. You might like to review the risky situations you listed on page 120 to help select one. See if you can develop a plan to prevent the imagined or real risk from occurring.

Identify the risky situation

....

List any advance planning or preparation

....

....

Discuss concerns and risks

....

....

Select risk-reduction strategies using problem-solving method

....

....

List rewards for appropriate behaviour

....

....

List back-up consequences for problem behaviour

....

....

List information/items required to make the plan work

....

....

When you plan a routine for a future event it is important to go through these steps together with your teenager. They need to learn how to do this too.

family survival tips

A lot of information has been presented so far in the program about strategies for managing teenagers' behaviour. However, it is easier to look after your teenager's needs if you also look after your own. Here are some more ideas that can help make parenting easier.

work as a team

Parenting is easier when both parents (where applicable) and other caregivers agree on methods of discipline. Parents should support and back up each other's parenting efforts. Before you use new strategies, discuss the plan with your partner and consult your teenager.

avoid arguments in front of your teenager

All children are very sensitive to adult conflict. They become distressed if arguments occur often and are not resolved. If you have a major disagreement, try to discuss it at a time when your teenager is not present. Parents sometimes think that teenagers are not affected by parental conflict, but they usually just show it less, or in unexpected ways.

If these issues are not addressed and resolved, it can cause considerable problems for teenagers, especially in developing their own relationships.

get support

Everyone needs support in raising teenagers. Partners, family, friends and neighbours can provide good support. Talk about your ideas and compare experiences. This is particularly important with teenagers. Parents are often unsure about how much freedom to allow, and can be swayed by comments like – *All my friends' parents are letting them go to the party!* This may be true – and it may not. Take the time to ring a few parents and find out. If you do not know any parents of your teenager's friends, make it your business to get to know them, at least so you can telephone occasionally and check out claims like these.

It is also important to be confident about where your teenager is, and what they are doing. Teenagers need to earn their parents' trust, and it is quite appropriate for parents to check on what they are told. Telephoning the parents of the friend they are supposed to be spending the evening with, or asking for details of the movie or show they were supposed to be watching shows that you care about them. You need to know where they are in case something goes wrong and they do not come home on time, or if you need to contact them over an emergency. As trust is demonstrated, you will need to check less, but this should not be taken for granted. Teenagers often get into trouble because they did not anticipate what might happen in a new situation. Having their parents know where they are can be a vital factor in avoiding serious problems.

If you know the parents of some of your teenager's friends, you are in a better position to monitor your teenager's behaviour. Monitoring does not need to be a big deal or a threat to your teenager's independence. It needs to be a natural part of your problem solving, risk-management planning. For example, when told initially about a daughter's plan to spend an evening with a friend, you might say: *Sounds fine. I'll just phone her mum and make sure it's okay with them* or *Okay. I'll give you a call around 9 p.m. to see how you're going to get home.*

Monitoring your teenager needs to be carried out in a matter-of-fact way. It tells your teenager you care about them and want to know what they are doing. As your teenager demonstrates that they are truthful, that their friends are reliable, and they are able to stick to planned arrangements, the need for monitoring may lessen, but it should never vanish completely as new situations will arise that pose new risks. You will need to make new plans to monitor these new situations as they arise.

have a break

Everyone needs some time away from their teenagers. This is normal and healthy. As your teenagers become more skilled and trustworthy, you will be able to leave them at home alone, or with friends, perhaps for an evening at first, and later for longer periods. A discreet telephone call to the house or to the neighbours may be used to reassure yourself that all is well. If things do not quite go as well as you hoped, impose an appropriate consequence, problem solve how to do it better next time, and then provide another opportunity at an appropriate time.

■ exercise 4 developing a parent and community network

Who do you rely on for support?

☐ family   ☐ friends

Write down the contact details of one person you could talk to or telephone at least once a week.

....

Write down the name, identity, and phone number of anyone else you know who you could contact for extra support or who could help you to monitor your teenager (e.g. friend's parent, youth worker, teacher).

NAME	IDENTITY / POSITION	PHONE NUMBER(S)

Make a note of things you like to do (on your own or with your partner or friends). The list on page 43 might provide some ideas.

....

....

Plan to have a break over the next week and decide who you can call on for help with this. Write down when you will do these things.

....

....

summary

This week you were introduced to the steps for planning a parenting routine for risky situations:

- do some advanced planning or preparation
- talk about concerns and risks
- select risk-reduction strategies
- use rewards to encourage appropriate behaviour
- use back-up consequences for problem behaviour
- obtain information/items required to make the plan work
- hold a follow-up discussion

In addition, family survival tips were introduced to help make the task of parenting easier.

practice tasks

- Write down the risky situation you plan to work on this week.

....

- Hold another family meeting (see example agenda on page 129).
- During the family meeting, review your behaviour contracts. There is a blank monitoring chart on page 132. Then develop a routine for the risky situation you selected above. There is a blank 'Dealing with risky behaviour routine' form on page 130, and an evaluation checklist on page 131.

  To complete the evaluation checklist, write down any problems or difficulties you had with any of the steps of your routine and whether the steps helped in reducing the risk. Additional copies of these checklists are provided in the Worksheets section.

- Continue to keep track of your teenager's behaviour. At this point you need to decide whether to continue monitoring the same behaviour. Use your behaviour graph to aid your decision. A useful guide is to stop monitoring once the behaviour has reached a satisfactory level and maintained at that level for at least five consecutive days. You may then wish to begin monitoring another target behaviour.

For a review of the material covered in today's session, you may like to watch:

- *Every Parent's Guide to Teenagers,* Part 5, Dealing with Risky Behaviour.

week 7

content of next week

Weeks 8 and 9 are designed to help you continue to put into practice routines for dealing with risky behaviour introduced this week. You will be encouraged to continue to design and implement planning ahead routines for risky situations, evaluate the success of your routines and refine them as necessary.

example agenda for family meeting

Preparation

- agree on time and place for meeting; agree on realistic time-limit (e.g. 30 minutes)
- gather all relevant material together (e.g. monitoring charts for behaviour contract/s, dealing with risky behaviour sheet)
- appoint chairperson, timekeeper, and recorder

Agenda

- *item 1:* review Behaviour Contract #1 for improving desirable behaviours and agree on any changes as necessary
- *item 2:* review Behaviour Contract #2 for reducing problem behaviours and agree on any changes as necessary
- *item 3:* negotiate and plan risky behaviour routine
- *item 4:* any other business
- *item 5:* set time for next meeting

Before closing the meeting, quickly review any important decisions that have been made.

Afterwards

Where possible, organise some brief pleasant activity for all family members to do together to reward everyone for taking part in the family meeting.

week 7

dealing with risky behaviour

Identify the risky situation

....

List any advance planning or preparation

....

....

....

Discuss concerns and risks

....

....

....

Select risk reduction strategies using problem-solving method

....

....

....

List rewards for appropriate behaviour

....

....

List backup consequences for problem behaviour

....

....

List information/items required to make plan work

....

....

After the event: note any goals from the follow-up discussion

....

....

checklist for dealing with risky behaviour routine

Risky situation: ....

Instructions: Write down any problems you encountered working through the routine with your teenager. Then write down opposite, whether the steps helped to reduce the risk.

STEPS FOLLOWED	COMMENTS
1. Advanced planning	
2. Discussing concerns and risks	
3. Selecting risk-reduction strategies	
4. Rewards	
5. Back-up consequences	
6. Information/items required	
7. New goals	

week 7

monitoring chart

Name: .... Week beginning: ....

ACTIVITY & DETAILS	CARRY OVER	M	T	W	T	F	S	S	TOTAL
Maximum points/day = • • • • • •									
Points lost per day Points earned per day Points available Points used Points remaining/carried									
Daily Rewards • • • • • • Weekly rewards • • • • • •									

implementing planning ahead routines 1

overview

The next two weeks are designed to help you put into practice the strategies introduced last week. Your main tasks this week are to review how successful your planning ahead routines for dealing with risky behaviour have been, refine them as necessary, and continue to design more routines for risky situations. You may be tempted to miss one or both of these weeks and move on to Week 10 – Program Close. This can work for some parents. However, it is important to recognise that it can take more than one trial of the routine for dealing with risky behaviour before this becomes a regular and effective approach to the wide range of situations where it can be useful. You may therefore find it difficult to help your teenager learn to manage risky situations if you do not practise using it a few more times.

By the end of Week 8 you should be able to:

- Plan, use and monitor routines to assist your teenager to deal with potentially risky situations.
- Access and use information on parenting issues if needed.
- Obtain support from family or friends when needed.

review of planning ahead routine to deal with risky behaviour

■ exercise 1 reviewing your use of the planning ahead routine to deal with risky behaviour

What were your practice tasks from last week (refer to page 128)?

....

....

....

What worked? Please be specific and think of at least two positive points. It may be helpful to look at your Checklist for Dealing with Risky Behaviour Routine (page 130).

....

....

....

Is there anything you could have done differently? You may notice some steps on your checklist for dealing with risky behaviour routine that you missed or could improve.

....

....

....

You may like to write down any changes to the plan if the situation is likely to occur again. Alternatively, you and your teenager may need to arrange a time to develop a new plan.

....

....

....

further planning

■ exercise 2 planning for future risky situations

Spend a few minutes planning possible solutions to these two situations. Use the blank Planning Ahead Routine for Dealing With Risky Behaviour forms on the next two pages.

Imagine you have a 14-year-old who has been in trouble during the last three weekends at a team sport (e.g. basketball, baseball, cricket, soccer) for yelling at team mates and for throwing their bat or ball in anger if they messed up. You are worried they will be thrown off the team if their anger outbursts continue.

Imagine you have a 13-year-old who is being teased and possibly bullied at school. They do not appear to have any close friends and report that they are being excluded from social groups and activities. They are coming home after school very upset and often complain of feeling sick in the mornings before school. They seem to believe the situation is hopeless, and complain that no one will ever like them and that they will never be any good at anything.

planning ahead routine for dealing with risky behaviour

Identify the risky situation

A 14-year-old at risk of getting thrown off the team

List any advance planning or preparation

Discuss concerns and risks

Select risk reduction strategies using problem-solving method

List rewards for appropriate behaviour

List backup consequences for problem behaviour

List information/items required to make plan work

After the event: note any goals from the follow-up discussion

You may wish to refer to page 167 to check your ideas.

planning ahead routine for dealing with risky behaviour

Identify the risky situation

A 13-year-old being teased and possibly bullied at school

List any advance planning or preparation

Discuss concerns and risks

Select risk reduction strategies using problem-solving method

List rewards for appropriate behaviour

List backup consequences for problem behaviour

List information/items required to make plan work

After the event: note any goals from the follow-up discussion

You may wish to refer to page 168 to check your ideas.

■ exercise 3 identifying future risky situations

Now turn to future risky situations that might occur for your teenager.

Write down any events or situations which you think could occur in the coming days or weeks (e.g. starting something new, doing something on their own for the first time, having problems at school). You may wish to review your notes for Exercise 2 on page 120 for other ideas.

List them below.

....

....

....

....

....

....

■ exercise 4 discuss a planning ahead routine with your teenager

Finally, do some planning of your own.

Select one of the situations you listed in Exercise 3 that is likely to occur this week or quite soon. Arrange a time to meet with your teenager to discuss how to help manage the situation. Use the blank form on page 139 to record your plan together.

planning ahead routine for dealing with risky behaviour

Identify the risky situation

....

List any advance planning or preparation

....

....

....

Discuss concerns and risks

....

....

....

Select risk reduction strategies using problem-solving method

....

....

....

List rewards for appropriate behaviour

....

....

List backup consequences for problem behaviour

....

....

List information/items required to make plan work

....

....

After the event: note any goals from the follow-up discussion

....

....

summary of activities

List the main points that came up this week that require follow-up by you.

....

....

....

....

....

....

- Ask your teenager to follow what was agreed during your use of the planning ahead routine in Exercise 4 (page 138) if the opportunity arises during the week. There is a blank Checklist for Dealing with Risky Behaviour Routine on page 141. An additional copy of this form is included in the Worksheets section. Make sure you hold a follow-up review with your teenager after the event.

- Continue to keep track of your teenager's behaviour. At this point you need to decide whether to continue monitoring the same behaviour. Use your behaviour graph to aid your decision. A useful guide is to stop monitoring once the behaviour has reached a satisfactory level and maintained at that level for at least five consecutive days. You may then wish to begin monitoring another target behaviour.

- Hold another family meeting to review progress.

For a review of the material covered in today's session, you may like to watch:

- *Every Parent's Guide to Teenagers,* Part 5, Dealing with Risky Behaviour.

content of next week

Week 9 gives you another opportunity to design and implement a planning ahead routine for risky behaviour, evaluate the success of your routines and refine them as necessary.

checklist for dealing with risky behaviour routine

Risky situation: ....

Instructions: Write down any problems you encountered working through the routine with your teenager. Then write down opposite, whether the steps helped to reduce the risk.

STEPS FOLLOWED	COMMENTS
1. Advanced planning	
2. Discussing concerns and risks	
3. Selecting risk-reduction strategies	
4. Rewards	
5. Back-up consequences	
6. Information/items required	
7. New goals	

week 8

implementing planning ahead routines 2

overview

This week is designed to help you continue to practise using planning ahead routines. You will review how successful your planning ahead routines for dealing with risky behaviour have been, refine them as necessary, and continue to design more routines for new situations. Alternatively, you may decide that you and your teenager are now regularly talking about how to manage new situations and using the planning steps quite comfortably. If this is the case you might prefer to move on to Week 10 – Program Close. However, if things are not going as well as you had hoped you might find it more valuable to complete Week 9 first. Before moving to Week 10 it is expected that your use of the planning ahead routine will have become a regular part of your discussions with your teenager.

By the end of Week 9 you should be able to:

- Plan, use and monitor routines to assist your teenager to deal with potentially risky situations.
- Access and use information on parenting issues if needed.
- Obtain support from family or friends when needed.

review of planning ahead routine to deal with risky behaviour

■ **exercise 1 reviewing your use of the planning ahead routine to deal with risky behaviour**

What were your practice tasks from last week (refer to page 140)?

....

....

....

What worked? Please be specific and think of at least two positive points. It may be helpful to look at your Checklist for Dealing with Risky Behaviour Routine (page 141).

....

....

....

Is there anything you could have done differently? You may notice some steps on your Checklist for Dealing with Risky Behaviour Routine that you missed or could improve.

....

....

....

You may like to write down any changes to the plan if the situation is likely to occur again. Alternatively, you and your teenager may need to arrange a time to develop a new plan.

....

....

....

further planning

■ exercise 2 planning for future risky situations

Spend a few minutes planning possible solutions to these two situations. Use the blank Planning Ahead Routine for Dealing With Risky Behaviour forms on the next two pages.

Imagine that the school holidays start in two weeks time, you have to work most of the time and you are concerned what your 13-year-old might get up to. You are also worried they will be bored and irritable and this will lead to more family squabbles and conflict.

Imagine you have a 14-year-old who complains that they are in danger of being excluded from their group of friends at school because you have said they cannot attend a late night party at a friend's home on the weekend. You are worried that the party will have alcohol and possibly drugs available and you are concerned that your teenager may give in to peer pressure and either drink heavily or try drugs. You do not want to restrict their social life but need a plan to reassure you that they will be okay.

planning ahead routine for dealing with risky behaviour

Identify the risky situation

A 13-year-old at home alone during the school holidays

List any advance planning or preparation

Discuss concerns and risks

Select risk reduction strategies using problem-solving method

List rewards for appropriate behaviour

List backup consequences for problem behaviour

List information/items required to make plan work

After the event: note any goals from the follow-up discussion

You may wish to refer to page 169 to check your ideas

planning ahead routine for dealing with risky behaviour

Identify the risky situation

A 14-year-old wanting to attend a late night party

List any advance planning or preparation

Discuss concerns and risks

Select risk reduction strategies using problem-solving method

List rewards for appropriate behaviour

List backup consequences for problem behaviour

List information/items required to make plan work

After the event: note any goals from the follow-up discussion

You may wish to refer to page 170 to check your ideas

exercise 3 identifying future risky situations

Now turn to future risky situations that might occur for your teenager.

Write down any events or situations which you think could occur in the coming days or weeks (e.g. starting something new, doing something on their own for the first time, having problems at school). You may wish to review your notes for Exercise 2 on page 120 for other ideas. List them below.

....

....

....

....

....

....

exercise 4 discuss a planning ahead routine with your teenager

Finally, do some planning of your own.

Use the blank form on page 149 to record your plan together. Select one of the situations you listed in Exercise 3 that is likely to occur this week or quite soon. Arrange a time to meet with your teenager to discuss how to help them manage the situation. Use the blank form on page 151 to record your plan together.

planning ahead routine for dealing with risky behaviour

Identify the risky situation

....

List any advance planning or preparation

....

....

....

Discuss concerns and risks

....

....

....

Select risk reduction strategies using problem-solving method

....

....

....

List rewards for appropriate behaviour

....

....

List backup consequences for problem behaviour

....

....

List information/items required to make plan work

....

....

After the event: note any goals from the follow-up discussion

....

....

summary of activities

List the main points that came up this week that require follow-up by you.

....

....

....

....

....

....

practice tasks

- Ask your teenager to follow what was agreed during your use of the planning ahead routine in Exercise 4 (page 148) if the opportunity arises during the week. There is a blank Checklist for Dealing with Risky Behaviour Routine on page 151. An additional copy of this form is included in the Worksheets section. Make sure you hold a follow-up review with your teenager after the event.

- Continue to keep track of your teenager's behaviour. At this point you need to decide whether to continue monitoring the same behaviour. Use your behaviour graph to aid your decision. A useful guide is to stop monitoring once the behaviour has reached a satisfactory level and maintained at that level for at least five consecutive days. You may then wish to begin monitoring another target behaviour.

- Hold another family meeting to review progress.

For a review of the material covered in today's session, you may like to watch:

- *Every Parent's Guide to Teenagers,* Part 5, Dealing with Risky Behaviour.

content of next week

Next week you will look at what has changed since you started Self-Help Teen Triple P and whether you have reached the goals you set at the beginning of the program. You will also be encouraged to think about how to keep things going after you have finished Teen Triple P.

checklist for dealing with risky behaviour routine

Risky situation: ....

Instructions: Write down any problems you encountered working through the routine with your teenager. Then write down opposite, whether the steps helped to reduce the risk.

STEPS FOLLOWED	COMMENTS
1. Advanced planning	
2. Discussing concerns and risks	
3. Selecting risk-reduction strategies	
4. Rewards	
5. Back-up consequences	
6. Information/items required	
7. New goals	

program close

overview

This is the last week of Self-Help Teen Triple P. You will review your family's progress through the program, and look at ways to maintain the changes you have made. If you think that you have not made as much progress as you had hoped to, you may wish to review some of the materials or exercises from earlier weeks. Perhaps you missed some of these or obstacles prevented you from going through them thoroughly. Keeping up improvements you have made over the longer term is important. Quality family life requires continued effort and you will need to be on the lookout for signs that things might be beginning to slip. You will also think about goals for the future and how to achieve these goals.

By the end of Week 10 you should be able to:

- Plan, use and monitor planning ahead routines to assist your teenager to deal with potentially risky situations.
- Obtain support from family and friends as well as from your parent support network.
- Solve parenting problems independently.

- Identify changes in your teenager's and your own behaviour since commencing Self-Help Teen Triple P.
- Maintain changes made so far in your teenager's and your own behaviour.
- Set further goals for change in your teenager's and your own behaviour and decide how to achieve these goals.

review of progress

▦ exercise 1 review use of strategies and routines

What were your practice tasks from last week (refer to page 150)?

....

....

What worked? Please be specific and think of at least two positive points. It may be helpful to look at your Checklist for Dealing with Risky Behaviour Routine (page 151).

....

....

Is there anything that you could have done differently? You may notice some steps on your checklist that you missed or could improve.

....

....

What might you need to practise further?

....

....

family survival tips

Take a few minutes to remember the family survival tips that were introduced in Week 7. These are covered in detail on pages 128 and 129. They are briefly listed here again:

- work as a team
- avoid arguments in front of your teenager
- get support
- have a break

■ exercise 2 taking care of yourself

Who do you rely on for support?

Family ....

....

Friends ....

....

What can you do to increase your support network, if needed?

....

....

....

....

Make a note of things you like to do (on your own or with your partner or friends) that you have not done for a while, or as regularly as you would like. The list on page 45 might provide some ideas.

....

....

....

....

Plan to have a break or do some of things you listed above. Write down when you will do this.

....

....

....

....

phasing out the program

During the course of this program, a number of things have been introduced into your family's life that are unusual – things that would probably not occur normally. Examples include practice tasks, keeping records of your own and your teenager's behaviour, and reading the program materials. Finishing a program like this involves phasing out these activities. However, this does not mean going back to all you were doing before starting the program. The aim at this stage is to phase out these unusual activities without falling back into the old patterns which were contributing to the problems you were experiencing with your teenager. A number of steps are suggested on the next page to help you do this.

put away the program materials

Put the program materials away somewhere so they are easy to find and you can pull them out to look at from time to time. You may choose to mark or take out those sections of the program materials that have been the most useful so they are easy to refer to.

phase out monitoring

Throughout the program you have been asked to keep records or to monitor what you have been doing and what your teenager has been doing. In everyday life, most people do not keep ongoing records of their own or their teenager's behaviour. If you are currently keeping records of your progress, decide how well established your new behaviours are. If you believe the new behaviour will now continue without keeping a record, it is time to stop recording. If you are less certain, start to phase out the recording. Monitor your own or your teenager's behaviour less often, such as once a week rather than each day, and aim to phase monitoring out altogether when you feel confident of your progress.

phase out specific strategies

Look at the type of strategies you have in place, such as behaviour contracts. Decide whether these can be simplified and phased out over time. Some of the suggestions we have made, such as praising a teenager frequently for a particular behaviour are most useful for changing behaviour. For maintaining behaviour it is best to reward behaviours unpredictably from time to time, and not every time the behaviour occurs.

Make changes to behaviour contracts and the use of rewards gradually. Make sure there are still plenty of rewarding things in your teenager's life, and that you look for opportunities to spend time together doing things that you both enjoy. Behaviour problems can reappear if teenagers do not get enough encouragement and support for appropriate behaviour.

hold regular reviews of progress

During this program, you have attended to your family's problems on a daily or weekly basis. This can be relaxed now. However, it is important to keep up with how your family is going. You might wish to keep the family meetings going once every two weeks or once a month. This allows you to review any problems that might be occurring and to address them before things become serious.

identifying changes

When you began Self-Help Teen Triple P, you identified goals for changes you wanted to see in your teenager's behaviour as well as in your own behaviour. To assist in identifying changes that have occurred since starting the program, you may wish to complete the Issues Checklist again. It will also give you a measure of whether you and your teenager are getting on better in relation to the specific issues you identified the first time you completed it in Week 1 (page 14). As you may recall, the Checklist contains a list of things that sometimes get talked about at home. Circle yes for the topics that you and your teenager have talked about at all during the last 4 weeks. Circle no for those topics that have not come up. Then where you have circled yes, circle the number on the right that best matches how hot your discussions on each topic have been. If both parents wish to complete the Checklist, either use different coloured pens, or use the spare copy in the Worksheets section.

issues checklist

Topic	Yes/No		Calm	A little angry			Angry
1. telephone calls	yes	no	1	2	3	4	5
2. time for going to bed	yes	no	1	2	3	4	5
3. cleaning up bedroom	yes	no	1	2	3	4	5
4. doing homework	yes	no	1	2	3	4	5
5. putting away clothes	yes	no	1	2	3	4	5
6. using the television or computer	yes	no	1	2	3	4	5
7. cleanliness (washing, showers, teeth)	yes	no	1	2	3	4	5
8. which clothes to wear	yes	no	1	2	3	4	5
9. how neat clothing looks	yes	no	1	2	3	4	5
10. making too much noise at home	yes	no	1	2	3	4	5
11. table manners	yes	no	1	2	3	4	5
12. fighting with brothers or sisters	yes	no	1	2	3	4	5
13. swearing or bad language	yes	no	1	2	3	4	5
14. how money is spent	yes	no	1	2	3	4	5
15. picking books or movies	yes	no	1	2	3	4	5
16. allowance/pocket money	yes	no	1	2	3	4	5
17. going places without parents (shopping, movies, etc.)	yes	no	1	2	3	4	5
18. playing music too loudly	yes	no	1	2	3	4	5
19. turning things off in the house (e.g. lights, TV, computer)	yes	no	1	2	3	4	5
20. drugs	yes	no	1	2	3	4	5
21. taking care of things (e.g. CDs, books, games, bikes, pets, etc.)	yes	no	1	2	3	4	5
22. drinking beer, wine, or other alcohol	yes	no	1	2	3	4	5
23. buying CDs, books, games, magazines	yes	no	1	2	3	4	5
24. going on dates	yes	no	1	2	3	4	5
25. who they should be friends with	yes	no	1	2	3	4	5
26. selecting new clothes	yes	no	1	2	3	4	5
27. sex	yes	no	1	2	3	4	5
28. coming home on time	yes	no	1	2	3	4	5
29. getting to school on time	yes	no	1	2	3	4	5
30. getting low grades in school	yes	no	1	2	3	4	5
31. getting in trouble in school	yes	no	1	2	3	4	5

week 10

Topic	Yes/No		Calm	A little angry			Angry
32. lying	yes	no	1	2	3	4	5
33. helping out around the home	yes	no	1	2	3	4	5
34. talking back to parents	yes	no	1	2	3	4	5
35. getting up in the morning	yes	no	1	2	3	4	5
36. bothering parents when they want to be left alone	yes	no	1	2	3	4	5
37. bothering teenager when he or she wants to be left alone	yes	no	1	2	3	4	5
38. putting feet on furniture	yes	no	1	2	3	4	5
39. messing up the house	yes	no	1	2	3	4	5
40. what time to have meals	yes	no	1	2	3	4	5
41. how to spend free time	yes	no	1	2	3	4	5
42. smoking	yes	no	1	2	3	4	5
43. earning money away from home	yes	no	1	2	3	4	5
44. what teenager eats	yes	no	1	2	3	4	5

To score your responses, first simply add up the number of times you circled yes. This should be a number between 0 and 44. Write your score here.

☐ A

Next, add up all the numbers you circled on the right. This should be a number between 0 and 220. Write this score here.

☐ B

Finally, divide the number in the lower box (B) by the number in the higher box (A). This will give you the average intensity of the discussions you had with your teenager. Write the answer here.

☐

For example, if you circled yes 20 times (higher box), and your intensity scores (lower box) totaled 40, your average intensity score will be 40/20 = 2.

This means that on a scale of 1 to 5, many of your discussions with your teenager appear to be quite calm, although there is still room for improvement. You can also use changes on the Checklist to identify specific issues with your teenager that have or have not improved, such as cleaning up their bedroom, helping around the house, or being more polite when they speak to you.

Remember, if you have scored **yes** more than 25 times, this suggests that you are experiencing more difficulty with your teenager than most parents do. Also, if your average intensity score (between 1 and 5) is higher than 2.2, this suggests that your discussions with your teenager are more angry than most parents experience. You may find it useful to compare these scores with your scores when you completed the Issues Checklist at the beginning of the program. If your scores are lower now than they were before, you have made some improvements. Well done! If they are not lower, or there are some particular issues that are still causing conflict, you may wish to consult with an accredited Teen Triple P provider to see whether some further assistance may be useful.

week 10

■ exercise 3 identifying changes that have been made

Take a few minutes to fill in the spaces below, outlining the changes that both you and your teenager have made since commencing the program. It may be helpful to look back at your goals on page 17.

CHANGES IN YOUR TEENAGER'S BEHAVIOUR	CHANGES IN YOUR OWN BEHAVIOUR

Congratulations on the changes you have made yourself and the changes you have helped your teenager to make.

maintaining changes

As this is the last week of Self-Help Teen Triple P, it is time to think about how to maintain all the changes you have made since starting the program. It has probably been hard work to achieve these changes. Your challenge now is to continue to work on preventing and managing new problems in the future. Here are some suggestions for maintaining the improvements you have made. There are five key steps to maintaining change and avoiding lapses.

identification of potential risky situations

An effective way of avoiding future problems involves using your new planning skills to deal with potentially difficult times before any trouble starts. This process can start now. Think of any risky situations that are likely to occur in the next few months and try to problem solve ways of dealing with these situations to minimise problems. Some common risky times include:

- changes in family structure (separation, new relationship, merging families)
- changes in family financial status
- changes in parental employment status
- times when parents are feeling depressed
- times of marital conflict
- moving house
- renovating or building a house
- changing schools
- exam times
- problems with friends, either same-sex or opposite-sex
- death or illness in the family
- involvement in court action

early identification of existing problems

It is important to take immediate action if things are not going well. You may decide to restart a specific management program such as a behaviour contract, or go back to the reading material to check strategies or look for new ideas.

hold regular reviews of progress

If you review your family's progress on a regular basis it is more likely that you will be able to detect any problems as they arise. You will also be able to take appropriate action to prevent any lapses. You may wish to keep the family meetings going to deal with regular events as well as problems. But in any case, review progress every two weeks at first, then at least once a month.

experiment with new strategies

If existing strategies are no longer effective, try out new things. Look to what you already know — give your teenager lots of attention and encouragement when they are behaving well and review how you are responding when they misbehave.

Try to find ways of adapting existing strategies to the new situation. Try out the new way for 10 to 14 days, monitor how successful it is, and continue or revise as appropriate.

talk to other parents

Do not feel you have to deal with issues on your own. Most parents of teenagers have similar problems, though not always at the same time or in the same order. Build up your network of parents so that everyone can benefit from each other's experiences and successes.

future goals

■ exercise 4 identifying future goals

Spend a few minutes now thinking about any other improvements you would like to see in your parenting skills and your teenager's behaviour. Remember to state your goals specifically.

....

....

....

summary

This week you have reviewed your progress through the program and the family survival tips that help make parenting easier. You also considered how to maintain the changes made, how to prevent problems in future high-risk situations, and you also set some goals for the future.

practice tasks

- Put your Teen Triple P materials away somewhere handy and start to phase out any monitoring records or checklists you may be using.
- Continue to use your positive parenting strategies and your parenting routines for risky situations.

Make a note of any other homework tasks or reading you intend to complete.

....

....

....

....

....

week 10

congratulations

You have now completed Self-Help Teen Triple P. Congratulations for staying motivated and interested throughout the program. We hope that you are enjoying the benefits of positive parenting and continue using these strategies. As your teenager continues to grow, different situations and new problems are bound to arise. Refer back to this Teen Triple P Self-Help Workbook at any time to review the strategies you have learned or to look up guidelines for dealing with a new problem behaviour. Congratulations for participating in Self-Help Teen Triple P. We hope you found it a worthwhile experience.

where to from here?

If you have completed Self-Help Teen Triple P and feel that you are still experiencing difficulties with your teenager's behaviour, your own feelings or your relationship with your partner, be prepared to seek professional help. Contact your family doctor, community health centre, school guidance officer or counsellor to find out where further help is available. You could also look on the Triple P website at www.triplep.net or look up psychology services in the telephone book.

week 10

answers to exercises

week 1

■ exercise 6 keeping track

Suggested monitoring forms for:

• How often a teenager swears at others.
Use a behaviour diary if the swearing occurs less than about five times per day, otherwise a tally sheet might be more appropriate. A parent may also choose to complete a tally sheet as well as a behaviour diary to help find out more about the triggers and consequences of the swearing. A duration record would not be appropriate given that swearing can occur in an instant. Unless the swearing occurs more than 15 times a day, a time sample would also be less useful.

• How long a teenager takes to complete homework each evening.
A duration record would show how long a teenager spends working on their homework each evening. The parent would have to be able to observe the teenager most of the time in order to be able to complete this record. Since the behaviour typically occurs once a day, a tally sheet would not be appropriate. However, if the parent can only check on the teenager occasionally, a modified time sampling record may be suitable where the parent checks the teenager (say) every ten

minutes and records an 'X' if the teenager is NOT studying.

- How often a teenager fights with brothers or sisters, particularly after school or before the evening meal.

Given that fighting is a behaviour that sometimes goes on and off, it is not always possible to tell when one incident of fighting stops and another starts. Therefore a time sample may be most appropriate. One option involves breaking the period before the evening meal into 15-minute intervals and recording the presence or absence of fighting in each 15-minute interval. If the fighting occurs often, a tally sheet and behaviour diary would not be appropriate. Also a duration record is unlikely to be appropriate as fighting is often cyclic rather than continuous.

- How often a teenager helps around the house.

As this relates to a number of possibly different behaviours, a tally sheet is probably the best way to keep track. If the chores are concentrated in a particular time period (e.g. between coming home from school and the evening meal) a time-sampling method may be used but this will not indicate how many different chores are carried out as some may carry over from one time period to the next.

- How often a teenager answers back or uses a disrespectful tone of voice.

Depending upon how often this behaviour occurs, a behaviour diary (less than five times per day) or frequency tally (up to 15 times a day) or time sample (several times per hour) may be used. A duration record is not likely to be helpful for this behaviour as talking back comes and goes quickly.

week 2

exercise 9 how to coach problem-solving

- When your teenager asks you questions, particularly the common *How?* or *Why?* questions (e.g. *How can I find out what time the next bus goes to town?*).

You could say something like *Hmmm, where do you think we might be able to get that information from?* or *What do you think other people do when they want information like that?*

- When your teenager cannot think of the right word for something (e.g. *What's another way of saying someone is rude?*).

You could say something like *What might they be doing to show that they're being rude?... Yes you could say they were putting you down.*

- When your teenager is frustrated with an activity and asks for help (e.g. *I can't work out how to do this!*).

You could ask them to break it down into smaller steps, such as *What's the first thing you need to do?* or ask if they know where clues might be found, such as *Is there a clue in your text book on this topic?*

week 3

exercise 4 making clear calm requests

- Your teenager's TV time allocation is used up but they continue to watch it.

Jason, you've watched TV for the time we agreed, please turn it off now.

- Your teenager is interrupting your telephone call by turning the TV up quite loud.

Mark, I can't hear on the telephone because the TV is too loud – please turn it down until I've finished with the call.

- Your teenager's wet towels and swimsuit are scattered on the floor.

Jackie, please pick up your towel and swimsuit and... hang them out to dry /... put them in the washing machine.

- Your teenager is yelling at a younger sibling to return something they borrowed.

Leeanne, stop yelling at your brother – speak quietly and politely.

- Your teenager is eating a snack in front of the TV and food scraps are being spilled on to the carpet.

Kelly, please pick up the food scraps from the floor and go to the table to eat.

Avoid using the following words and phrases when making requests:

Would you like to ...?
Can you ... ?
I want you to ... ?
How about you ... ?
Do you want to ... ?
It would make me happy if you ... ?

These are all examples of vague requests as they do not clearly indicate to your teenager exactly what they need to do. When requests are phrased as questions, teenagers have a choice and can say *No*. Requests which are merely statements of what parents would like or want do not make it clear that action is required.

■ exercise 5 backing up your requests with logical consequences

- Your teenager is playing music too loudly and has not followed your request to turn it down.

Turn off the music for 15 to 30 minutes (e.g. *You haven't turned the music down as I asked – now I'm going to turn it off for 15 minutes*).

- Your teenager has borrowed their brother's computer game without permission and ignores your request that they should go and ask him.

Turn the computer game off and remove the game / disk if possible (e.g. *You haven't asked your brother's permission to borrow that game as I asked – the computer is going off for 30 minutes and give me the disk*). Do not allow your teenager to avoid the consequence by saying they will go and ask their brother now – the consequence is for not following your initial request. They will still need to ask their brother before they are given the disk back, but the 30 minutes computer turn off is for not doing what you asked.

answers to exercises

- Your teenager is arguing loudly with a sibling about which TV channel to watch, and ignores your suggestion that they solve the problem in a friendly and quiet way.

Turn off the TV for 15 to 30 minutes (e.g. *You haven't been able to decide quietly which program to watch so the TV is going off for 15 minutes*). You may also want to prompt them to problem solve to avoid a repetition of the arguing when the TV is turned back on (e.g. *I suggest you spend that time discussing how you can share the TV. Any ideas?*).

- Your teenager borrowed your bike, and despite your request that they put it away, has left it out in the rain.

If you know they plan to use the bike again soon, make it unavailable (e.g. *You haven't put my bike away as I asked – now you can't use it for the next hour*). If you think they don't want to use the bike again, you may need to find another related consequence (e.g. *You're watching TV instead of putting my bike away as I asked so the TV is going off for 30 minutes*). If your teenager goes and puts the bike away immediately, do not return the TV until the 30 minutes is up. The consequence is for not doing as you asked the first time. Do not apply a consequence that requires the teenager to do something else (e.g. *You didn't put my bike away as I asked so now I want you to go and clean it and dry it and put it away*). If they refuse you now have to deal with two instances of their ignoring your request. Also, do not make the length of the consequence dependent on putting the bike away as your teenager may turn it into a contest to see who gives in first (e.g. *You can't watch TV again until you put my bike away!*).

▓ exercise 6 preparing to deal calmly with teenagers' emotions

- What can you say to your teenager when you notice they are distressed about something?

Tell me what you're upset about; Hey, you look really upset; Do you want to tell me what's happened?

- What can you say to your teenager to show you are listening?

Sit down and tell me about it; I'm listening; OK tell me what happened.

- What can you say to your teenager to show you understand that they are feeling emotional?

You sound really angry; You must be really upset about that; I can see you're really mad about that.

- When can you ask your teenager if you can help?

Only after you've listened and acknowledged how they're feeling and only if they've calmed down a bit (e.g. *Is there anything I can do? Do you want my help to try and find a solution?*).

- What can you say to your teenager if they have calmed down and want you to help them sort things out?

What do you think you might do?; What are your options here?; How do you want it to be different?

- What could you say to your teenager if they have not calmed down or do not want your help?

You still seem really upset — how about we take some time out and talk about it later?; I don't think it's a good idea to discuss this now while we're both getting a bit uptight — when would be a good time to talk?; I'm going to go and take the dog for a walk — how about we talk about it when I get back and we've both calmed down?

◼ exercise 8 preparing to deal with manipulative behaviour

- What can you say to your teenager when you notice them complain they cannot do something you know they can?

What are you finding difficult? How about breaking it down into smaller steps? How about I help you get started?

- What can you say to your teenager if they ask you to do something that they should really do for themselves?

That's something you have to do yourself; You need to learn how to do that; I'll help you work out how to begin.

- What can you say to your teenager if they shout at you that you should fix their problem for them?

Losing your temper won't solve this problem; You need to be calm to work this through; Take a few minutes to calm down and then I'll help you make a start.

week 8

◼ exercise 2 planning for future risky situations

example routine for dealing with risky behaviour
A 14-year-old at risk of getting thrown off the team

Identify the risky situation

- Losing their temper and assaulting or injuring another team member; being suspended or excluded from the team

List any advanced planning or preparation

- Talk to coach to discover more about the situation
- Watch a game to observe what goes on

Talk about concerns and risks

- Losing temper can lead to many relationship problems, with friends, at school, and at work
- It may result in getting into fights, being injured, or injuring someone else

Select risk reduction strategies

- Monitor thoughts and feelings about other players, referee, spectators
- Identify what happens just before losing temper
- Take several deep breaths; say "keep calm" to self

- Talk to coach about coming off for a brief period of 'time out' when things begin to get out of control

Agree on reward for appropriate behaviour

- Tickets to watch a professional or league game
- Points toward new sporting clothes or equipment
- Autograph from sporting hero

Specify a back-up consequence for problem behaviour

- Miss out on professional or league game
- Miss social or other event connected with team activity
- Have to miss a game

List information/items required to make the plan work

- Inform coach of plan
- Make sure rewards can be provided as promised

Hold a follow-up discussion

- After the game, review how the plan worked
- Revise the plan if extra strategies are needed
- Praise any improvements in behaviour

example routine for dealing with risky behaviour

A 13-year-old being teased and possibly being bullied at school

Identify the risky situation

- Being teased or bullied by other students on the way to and from school, during a break, and on the way to and from classes

List any advanced planning or preparation

- Talk to staff at school to discuss school policy on bullying and to find which staff are responsible for putting it into practice
- Talk to other parents (if possible) to find out if they are also concerned

Talk about concerns and risks

- Teasing and bullying can lead to increased social isolation, a loss of self-esteem, not wanting to go to school, and school work suffering
- It may also result in getting into arguments or fights, being injured, or injuring someone else, and possibly being suspended from school

Select risk reduction strategies

- Identify places and people where teasing or bullying is more/less likely
- Identify other students to make friends with
- Where possible, keep in a group; don't get isolated

- If teasing or bullying occurs, take several deep breaths; say "keep calm" to self
- Talk to designated staff member if matters get out of control

Agree on reward for appropriate behaviour

- Spend more time with new friends on weekend
- Points toward new clothes or magazine, etc
- Go to special social event with a friend

Specify a back-up consequence for problem behaviour

- Miss out on points toward new clothes, etc.

List information/items required to make the plan work

- Inform teenager of responsible teacher to contact and where to find them
- Perhaps ask other parents to encourage their teenagers to provide support

Hold a follow-up discussion

- After each day, review how the plan worked
- Revise the plan if extra strategies are needed
- Praise any improvements in dealing with teasing or bullying

week 9

▨ exercise 2 planning for future risky situations

example routine for dealing with risky behaviour

A 13-year-old at home alone during school holidays

Identify the risky situation

- Being at home alone, getting bored and irritable, watching too much TV and lazing around

List any advanced planning or preparation

- Ask friends what they are planning to do in the holidays before school finishes and obtain their telephone numbers
- Make some arrangements to telephone friends and/or to meet up
- Check the local library, newspaper, etc to find out what activities might be on in the holidays
- Make sure teenager earns pocket money in advance to spend during the holiday period

Talk about concerns and risks

- Sitting at home alone watching TV will make teenager bored, listless and irritable
- Extra pressure and stress on parent to make things happen

Select risk reduction strategies

- Telephone friends each evening to organise activities for coming days
- Plan the week to avoid one day just drifting into the next
- Arrange regular contact with parent each day to keep them informed of what's happening
- Arrange transport where necessary to help take part in activities
- Lock TV or cables away to prevent excessive TV watching

Agree on reward for appropriate behaviour

- Time together with parent in evening or on weekend doing something teenager enjoys
- TV time or a DVD in the evening

Specify a back-up consequence for problem behaviour

- Miss out on TV in evening
- Have to go with parent to work (if possible)
- Have to go to stay with grandparent or other family member for supervision

List information/items required to make the plan work

- Addresses and telephone numbers of friends
- Telephone number of parent's work place

Hold a follow-up discussion

- After each day/week, review how the plan worked
- Revise the plan if extra strategies are needed
- Praise any activities that are appropriate

example routine for dealing with risky behaviour

A 14-year-old wanting to attend a late-night party

Identify the risky situation

- Having someone put something in their drink or drinking to excess, and getting involved in undesirable sexual activity

List any advanced planning or preparation

- Talk to parents where party is to be held to discover more about supervision at the party
- Find out who else is likely to attend (e.g. age range, numbers)

Talk about concerns and risks

- Getting drugged or drunk and being persuaded or tempted to go into a bedroom with someone
- It may result in unsafe sex (possible pregnancy or sexually transmitted diseases)

Select risk reduction strategies

- Decide ahead of time what drinks are acceptable – take your own if necessary and don't accept drinks from anyone else, especially drinks that have already been opened
- Agree to stay with a friend to watch each other's drinks and provide support to each other
- Don't go off alone, especially where no one else is around
- Agree on what time they must leave the party and organise how they will get home
- Agree that they will not let anyone else bring them home without first checking with parent

Agree on reward for appropriate behaviour

- Being able to go to another party
- New clothes or accessories
- Special outing with parent to an activity or event that the teenager enjoys

Specify a back-up consequence for problem behaviour

- Not allowed to go to the next party
- Miss out on special outing

List information/items required to make the plan work

- Telephone number and address of house where the party is taking place
- Clear agreement about rules to be followed and arrangements for coming home

Hold a follow-up discussion

- After the party, review how the plan worked
- Revise the plan for next time if extra strategies are needed
- Praise any behaviour that made the evening safe and enjoyable

worksheets

It is intended that you will make multiple copies of the following worksheets to use with the exercises in your workbook. Remember to keep the originals so you can make additional copies as required.

behaviour diary

Instructions: List the problem behaviour, when and where it happened and what happened before and after.

Problem behaviour: ....

Day: ....

PROBLEM	WHEN AND WHERE DID IT HAPPEN?	WHAT HAPPENED BEFORE?	WHAT HAPPENED AFTER?	OTHER COMMENTS

worksheets

tally sheet

Instructions: Write the day in the first column, then place a tick in the next column each time the behaviour occurs on that day. Record the total number of ticks for each day in the end column.

Behaviour: ....

Start Date: ....

DAY	1	2	3	4	5	6	7	8	9	10	11	12	13	14	15	TOTAL

duration record

Instructions: Write the day in the first column, then for each separate occurence of the target behaviour, record how long it lasted in seconds, minutes or hours. Total the times at the end of each day.

Behaviour: .... Start Date: ....

DAY	SUCCESSIVE EPISODES										TOTAL

time-sampling record

Instructions: Place a tick in the square for the corresponding time period if the target behaviour has occurred at least once.

Behaviour: ....   Start Date: ....

DAYS	M	T	W	T	F	S	S	M	T	W	T	F	S	S	M	T	W	T	F	S	S

TIME OF DAY

behaviour graph

Instructions: Plot the number of times the behaviour happens each day by placing a cross on the appropriate column, then join up the marks for each day.

Behaviour: ....

Month: ....

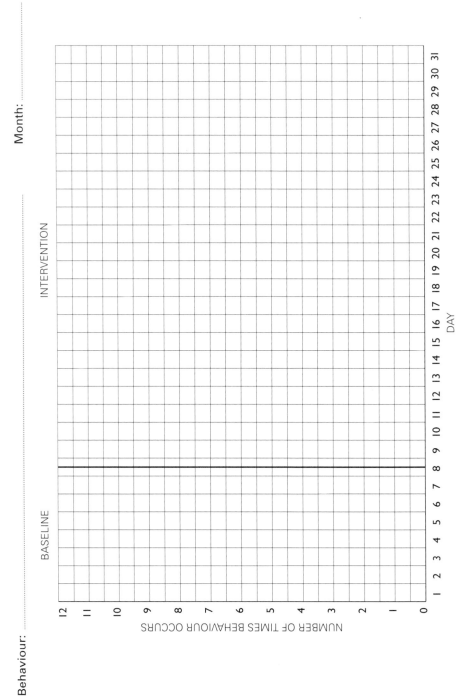

checklist for encouraging appropriate behaviour / managing problem behaviour

Choose two strategies that you would like to practise with your teenager over the next week. Be as specific as possible (e.g. one goal may be to use descriptive praise statements with your teenager at least three times per day). Use the table below to record whether you reached your goals each day. Comment on what went well and list any problems that occurred.

GOAL 1:

....

....

GOAL 2:

....

....

DAY	GOAL 1 Y/N	GOAL 2 Y/N	COMMENTS
1			
2			
3			
4			
5			
6			
7			

worksheets

practice task checklist

Day: ....

Time: between .... and ....

Note down your goals for this week's practice task/s. Be as specific as possible (e.g. one goal may be to use logical consequences with your teenager when they don't cooperate with your requests). Use the table below to record whether you reach your goals or not. Comment on what went well and list any problems that occurred. If there is no opportunity to practise a task on the selected day, pick another day later in the week and try again.

GOAL 1:

....

....

GOAL 2:

....

....

GOAL 3:

....

....

	GOALS ACHIEVED Y/N	COMMENTS
GOAL 1:		
GOAL 2:		
GOAL 3:		

worksheets

planning ahead routine for dealing with risky behaviour

Identify the risky situation

....

List any advance planning or preparation

....

....

....

Discuss concerns and risks

....

....

....

Select risk reduction strategies using problem-solving method

....

....

....

List rewards for appropriate behaviour

....

....

List backup consequences for problem behaviour

....

....

List information/items required to make plan work

....

....

After the event: note any goals from the follow-up discussion

....

....

checklist for dealing with risky behaviour routine

Risky situation: ....

Instructions: Write down any problems you encountered working through the routine with your teenager. Then write down opposite, whether the steps helped to reduce the risk.

STEPS FOLLOWED	COMMENTS
1. Advanced planning	
2. Discussing concerns and risks	
3. Selecting risk-reduction strategies	
4. Rewards	
5. Back-up consequences	
6. Information/items required	
7. New goals	

monitoring chart

Name: .... Week beginning: ....

ACTIVITY & DETAILS	CARRY OVER	M	T	W	T	F	S	S	TOTAL
Maximum points/day = • • • • • •									
Points lost per day Points earned per day Points available Points used Points remaining/carried									
Daily Rewards • • • • • • Weekly rewards • • • • • •									

Additional conditions/comments

....

....

issues checklist

Circle yes for the topics that you and your teenager have talked about at all during the last 4 weeks. Circle no for those topics that have not come up. Then where you have circled yes circle the number on the right that best matches how hot your discussions have been.

Topic	Yes/No		Calm	A little angry			Angry
1. telephone calls	yes	no	1	2	3	4	5
2. time for going to bed	yes	no	1	2	3	4	5
3. cleaning up bedroom	yes	no	1	2	3	4	5
4. doing homework	yes	no	1	2	3	4	5
5. putting away clothes	yes	no	1	2	3	4	5
6. using the television or computer	yes	no	1	2	3	4	5
7. cleanliness (washing, showers, teeth)	yes	no	1	2	3	4	5
8. which clothes to wear	yes	no	1	2	3	4	5
9. how neat clothing looks	yes	no	1	2	3	4	5
10. making too much noise at home	yes	no	1	2	3	4	5
11. table manners	yes	no	1	2	3	4	5
12. fighting with brothers or sisters	yes	no	1	2	3	4	5
13. swearing or bad language	yes	no	1	2	3	4	5
14. how money is spent	yes	no	1	2	3	4	5
15. picking books or movies	yes	no	1	2	3	4	5
16. allowance/pocket money	yes	no	1	2	3	4	5
17. going places without parents (shopping, movies, etc.)	yes	no	1	2	3	4	5
18. playing music too loudly	yes	no	1	2	3	4	5
19. turning things off in the house (e.g. lights, TV, computer)	yes	no	1	2	3	4	5
20. drugs	yes	no	1	2	3	4	5
21. taking care of things (e.g. CDs, books, games, bikes, pets, etc.)	yes	no	1	2	3	4	5
22. drinking beer, wine, or other alcohol	yes	no	1	2	3	4	5
23. buying CDs, books, games, magazines	yes	no	1	2	3	4	5
24. going on dates	yes	no	1	2	3	4	5
25. who they should be friends with	yes	no	1	2	3	4	5
26. selecting new clothes	yes	no	1	2	3	4	5
27. sex	yes	no	1	2	3	4	5
28. coming home on time	yes	no	1	2	3	4	5
29. getting to school on time	yes	no	1	2	3	4	5
30. getting low grades in school	yes	no	1	2	3	4	5
31. getting in trouble in school	yes	no	1	2	3	4	5
32. lying	yes	no	1	2	3	4	5
33. helping out around the home	yes	no	1	2	3	4	5

worksheets

34. talking back to parents	yes	no	1	2	3	4	5
35. getting up in the morning	yes	no	1	2	3	4	5
36. bothering parents when they want to be left alone	yes	no	1	2	3	4	5
37. bothering teenager when he or she wants to be left alone	yes	no	1	2	3	4	5
38. putting feet on furniture	yes	no	1	2	3	4	5
39. messing up the house	yes	no	1	2	3	4	5
40. what time to have meals	yes	no	1	2	3	4	5
41. how to spend free time	yes	no	1	2	3	4	5
42. smoking	yes	no	1	2	3	4	5
43. earning money away from home	yes	no	1	2	3	4	5
44. what teenager eats	yes	no	1	2	3	4	5

To score your responses, first simply add up the number of times you circled yes. This should be a number between 0 and 44. Write your score here ☐ A

Next, add up all the numbers you circled on the right. This should be a number between 0 and 220. Write this score here ☐ B

Finally, divide the number in the lower box (B) by the number in the higher box (A). This will give you the average intensity of the discussions you had with your teenager. Write the answer here ☐

For example, if you circled yes 20 times (higher box), and your intensity scores (lower box) totaled 40, your average intensity score will be 40/20 = 2.

This means that on a scale of 1 to 5, many of your discussions with your teenager appear to be quite calm, although there is still room for improvement. You can also use changes on the Checklist to identify specific issues with your teenager that have or have not improved, such as cleaning up their bedroom, helping around the house, or being more polite when they speak to you.

Remember, if you have scored **yes** more than 25 times, this suggests that you are experiencing more difficulty with your teenager than most parents do. Also, if your average intensity score (between 1 and 5) is higher than 2.2, this suggests that your discussions with your teenager are more angry than most parents experience. You may find it useful to compare these scores with your scores when you completed the Issues Checklist at the beginning of the program. If your scores are lower now than they were before, you have made some improvements. Well done! If they are not lower, or there are some particular issues that are still causing conflict, you may wish to consult with an accredited Teen Triple P provider to see whether some further assistance may be useful.

The Issues Checklist is reproduced with the permission of Dr. Ronald J. Prinz

notes